ChatGPT For Beginners Over Fifty

The Complete Guide to Prompt Mastery – Save Time, Boost Productivity & Monetize Your Best Ideas with Ease

Margaret Fields

1957 Publishing

This Book Belongs To

FREE
BONUS
CHAPTER
365
Prompts
FREE

Cover Design by: Margaret Fields

About The Author

Margaret Fields

At 68 years young, Margaret Fields is a proud senior, a devoted mother of three, and a loving grandmother to four.

Her journey began at St Patrick's Business College, where she was named Dux at just 17 years old. Over the decades, Margaret has witnessed firsthand the transformation of technology – from the arrival of electric golf-ball typewriters in the 1970s to her awe at IBM's Memory Typewriter in 1977. Her curiosity only deepened with her first computer in the mid-90s and again in 2011, when her business brought Australia's first 7-axis robotic stone milling machine to market.

Armed with a Master of Arts with Excellence from the University of New South Wales and proudly identifying as a neurodivergent thinker, Margaret brings both empathy and clarity to her work. Her passion lies in making today's technology feel welcoming, empowering, and even a little fun – especially for those who didn't grow up with it.
This book continues her mission to help others confidently navigate the digital age, one friendly prompt at a time.

Dedication

My Stubborn & Independent Self

To my wonderfully stubborn, fiercely independent self -
the one who never waited for permission,
never quite fit the mold,
and never backed down from learning something new,
even when the tech tried to outwit her,

and even when others doubted her ability to succeed.

This book is for every curious click, every late-night "aha,"
and every moment you refused to be left behind,

proving wrong those who couldn't see what you were capable of.

Here's to doing it your way -
always.

There once was a curious blend,
Of coffee, of courage, and friend.
A café of thought,
Where wisdom was sought,
And tech met the will to transcend.

With brews poured beside every byte,
The questions came morning and night.
But laughter was steeped,
And learning ran deep,
In a space that just felt... right.

So pull up a chair, take a sip,
Let old doubts and worries slip.
This menu is made
For the bold, unafraid -
To give AI a confident tip!

Contents

Introduction	XIII
1. Understanding ChatGPT Basics	1
2. Practical Applications in Everyday Life	15
3. Bridging Generational Gaps	29
4. Enhancing Travel Experiences	45
Make A Difference	59
5. Lifelong Learning and Creativity	61
6. Safety and Privacy in the Digital Age	77
7. Interactive and Engaging Content	91
8. Empowerment and Exploration	107
Conclusion	121
References	125
ChatGPT Café Glossary of Terms	131
BONUS Chapter	135
Breadcrumbs	138

Introduction

Have you ever yelled "Why won't this jolly thing just listen to me?!" at your computer... only to realize it wasn't even turned on?... well I know just how you feel... guilty as charged on that one!

It was 1977, and I'd just started a new job – banished, as all the young newbies were, to a gloomy little office in the basement of a freight forwarding warehouse in Rydalmere. There, surrounded by dust and the low hum of industry, sat an IBM Memory Typewriter. It was brand new and had been left to sulk in the corner like a machine with a bad reputation – too complicated, clever, and misunderstood. No one wanted it. It had arrived way ahead of its time. Most had given up on it. But not me.

With nothing but a steaming coffee and a bar of Cadbury chocolate for company, I sat down and gave it a go. To my surprise, it wasn't intimidating – it was intuitive. Logical. Almost musical. Where others saw a foe, I found a friend. That machine sang for me, and I sang right back. It was as if it had been built with my brain in mind.

It took me from silly little newbie to Most Appreciated Assistant faster than you could say "carbon copy." Thanks to its 100 memory sections, I looked like I was doing the work of three people - while secretly sipping tea and humming to ABBA. No one could figure out how I was so productive. I wasn't about to spill the beans. This new typewriter and I? We had an unspoken agreement.

That moment was an unexpected win that quietly rewired how I saw myself and technology. I didn't just keep up; I found my rhythm.

Hi, I'm Margaret Fields – mother of three, grandmother of four, and now 68 years young. I've witnessed first-hand technology leap from golf-ball typewriters to the magic of robots and ChatGPT. I'm still just as curious as I was in that dusty basement.

Now, you might be thinking, "ChatGPT? Isn't that just for the younger generation?" Well, let me tell you, my friend, that couldn't be further from the truth! In fact, a recent survey found that 70% of adults over 50 are eager to learn new technologies to stay connected with family and friends. And that's where this book comes in.

"ChatGPT For Beginners Over Fifty" is your ticket to a new world of possibilities. It's not just about learning how to use a fancy AI tool; it's about transforming your communication, boosting productivity, and bridging the generational gap. By the time you finish this book, you'll chat with your grandkids like a pro and impress your friends with your newfound tech-savvy skills.

But here's the real kicker: this book isn't just about mastering ChatGPT. It's about shifting the narrative around seniors in our society. Too often, we're seen as technologically challenged or stuck in the past. Well, I'm here to tell you that's a load of hogwash! This book will show you how to become a tech-savvy, socially relevant member of your community, proving that seniors have a vital role to play in our rapidly changing world.

Throughout these pages, we'll dive into the nitty-gritty of mastering prompting, leveraging AI for personal and family use, and fostering a lifelong love of learning. You'll learn to reduce downtime, increase productivity, and monetize your ideas. And the best part? We'll do it all with relatable examples, practical applications, beauty, and a sprinkle of humor.

Imagine being able to easily plan your dream vacation, thanks to ChatGPT's personalized recommendations. Or picture yourself having meaningful, in-depth conversations with your grandkids about their favorite topics, all because you know how to ask ChatGPT the right questions. The possibilities are endless, and they're all within your reach.

Yes, yes... I know what you might be thinking: "But hang on there, Margaret, I'm not a tech whiz like you!" Trust me, I've been there. As a neurodivergent thinker, I've had to teach myself the ins and outs of IT. I know firsthand how challenging it can be to find age-appropriate, structured learning materials. That's why I've poured my heart and soul into creating this book - to make the journey easier for you.

Learning something new – especially in the world of technology – can feel like sipping a strong espresso for the first time: bold, energizing, and maybe a little overwhelming.

For that very reason, throughout this book, you'll find little pauses called **Reader Reviver Brain Breaks**. Think of them as friendly café moments between the chapters - spaces to breathe, stretch your thoughts, and wander off track (on purpose).

Each break includes a hand-drawn Table Talk Card - the kind you might find waiting at your favorite local café, held up by something unexpected like a marble pear or a painted pebble. A reflective, whimsical, or gently surprising question is on the card - just enough to delightfully distract your mind.

These aren't quizzes. They're invitations. To reflect. To play. To reconnect with your curious self.

When you see one, pause for a moment. Refill your cup, rest your eyes, and let your thoughts do something completely unproductive. Because sometimes, that's where the best ideas live.

So, are you ready to embark on this transformative adventure? To embrace new possibilities and unlock your brain's full potential? Then buckle up, buttercup, because we are about to take a wild ride into ChatGPT!

But before we dive in, let me leave you with one final thought. This book isn't just about learning a new skill, empowering yourself, and embracing personal growth. It's about proving to yourself and the world that you're never too old to learn, grow, and make a difference.

Let's do this together. With an open mind, a willingness to explore, and a healthy dose of humor, there's no limit to what we can achieve. Welcome to "ChatGPT For Beginners Over Fifty," ... your ultimate guide to mastering prompting, reducing downtime, increasing productivity... and maximizing the monetization of your ideas. Let's show the world what we're made of!

Understanding ChatGPT Basics

Let me take you back to a time when my technological prowess was tested by the infamous IBM Memory Typewriter. It was clunky, loud, and intimidating, but oh my, the thrill of watching those keys dance under my fingertips. That machine was my first taste of technology's potential, and it set me on a path of discovery that led to many a tech triumph and a few hilarious mishaps. Fast forward to today, and technology has leaped forward in ways I could never have imagined. It's now less about clunky typewriters and more about sleek, smart tools like ChatGPT. But what exactly is ChatGPT? You might be picturing a tiny robot sitting on your shoulder, whispering sweet nothings in your ear. Alas, it's not quite that, but it's just as exciting and far more helpful.

What is ChatGPT? A Simple Explanation

At its core, ChatGPT is an AI language model. Let me break that down before you throw your hands up in despair. Think of it as that chatty friend who is always ready to help without needing tea or biscuits. This clever AI can generate human-like text responses, making it feel like you're conversing with someone who listens – unlike Uncle Bob at the dinner table. It's trained on a vast array of information, enabling it to understand and respond to your prompts with surprising accuracy. Whether planning a family event or drafting emails, ChatGPT can make these tasks feel less like chores and more like a fun challenge.

Let's talk practicality because that's what we're all about. Imagine you're planning a family reunion. You want everyone to have a good time, but coordinating all the details feels like herding cats. Enter ChatGPT. It can suggest activities, help draft invitations, and even provide tips for keeping the peace when Cousin Sally insists on bringing her karaoke machine. Or perhaps you're writing an email to a dear friend you haven't seen for quite a while. With ChatGPT, your words can flow more naturally, capturing the warmth and humor you'd share if you were face-to-face. It's your secret weapon for turning mundane tasks into moments of connection and creativity.

Now, I know technology can sometimes feel like it's designed by aliens for aliens, but ChatGPT prides itself on being user-friendly. Its interface is as straightforward as a Sunday drive, and you won't need a degree in computer science to navigate it. Simple commands mean you can jump right in, whether tech-savvy or not. This is a breath of fresh air for those who didn't grow up with smartphones glued to their hands. It's akin to having a GPS that doesn't insist on sending you through a cow field.

Of course, with all the hype, it's easy to get carried away and expect ChatGPT to solve world peace or find your lost socks. While it's an impressive tool, it does have its limits. ChatGPT is brilliant at generating text and providing information. Still, it's not a mind reader and won't find your socks. It doesn't understand context like humans do, so if asked to advise which grandchild is most likely to become an astronaut, it might not have the correct answer. It's also not a substitute for professional advice; for any serious matters, consult a real-life expert.

In short, ChatGPT is like the Swiss Army knife of conversation and creativity, ready to assist, entertain, and educate. It's here to make your life easier, not more complicated. So, let's dive into this world of AI together with a sense of adventure and that healthy dose of humor. And remember, even if it can't find your lost socks, ChatGPT is still a pretty nifty addition to your digital toolbox.

How ChatGPT Works: A Beginner's Insight

Imagine entering a bustling marketplace of words where every phrase and sentence is alive, ready to spring into action at your command. That's the magical realm of

ChatGPT, powered by the marvels of natural language processing and machine learning. These terms might sound daunting, but think of natural language processing as the art of teaching computers to understand our everyday chatter. It's like giving a computer the ability to listen to conversations and respond appropriately, much like a well-mannered dinner guest who knows when to laugh at your jokes.

Now, sprinkle in a bit of machine learning, which is essentially teaching computers to learn from data over time. Picture this: a young apprentice diligently studying all the books in a library to become wise and knowledgeable. That's what machine learning does for AI – it reads, learns, and evolves. ChatGPT is a product of this sophisticated dance, constantly refining its ability to predict what words come next in a sentence, just like a seasoned, improved actor who always knows the right line to keep the show going.

But how do you, dear reader, interact with such a marvel? It's simpler than you might think. Engaging with ChatGPT is like conversing with a delightfully patient friend who never tires of your questions. You start by inputting a prompt – anything from "What's the weather like in Sydney?" to something more philosophical like "What's the meaning of life?"—and watch as ChatGPT generates a response. It's as if you've turned on a faucet, and words flow forth, each carefully chosen to create coherent and often insightful replies.

The beauty of ChatGPT lies in its feedback loop. Much like a chef who adjusts a recipe based on diners' feedback, ChatGPT learns from interactions, refining its responses to better suit your needs. You might find it providing writing assistance, transforming a blank page into a canvas filled with your thoughts, or acting as a virtual travel guide, offering tips and trivia about your next holiday destination.

Now, let's address the elephant in the room: AI can feel a bit like a magic trick, too good to be true. Concerns about safety and privacy are valid and worth discussing. Rest assured, ChatGPT doesn't have a secret agenda. It operates within defined parameters to ensure user safety, incorporating measures like data anonymization to protect your privacy. You might think of it as a vigilant librarian, fiercely guarding the confidentiality of its patrons.

Regarding privacy, it's wise to treat ChatGPT like any online tool – share information thoughtfully and verify facts with reputable sources. While ChatGPT aims to be accurate, it's important to remember it's not infallible. It's a tool to augment your capabilities, not replace your intuition or professional advice. It's like a trusty sidekick, always ready to assist but never taking the lead in matters of critical importance.

Embrace ChatGPT for what it is: a helpful companion on your tech journey, ready to simplify, enhance, and enrich your digital interactions. Whether you're crafting a memorable toast for a family gathering or plotting your next great adventure, ChatGPT stands by, eager to lend a hand.

Setting Up ChatGPT: A Step-by-Step Visual Guide

Picture this: You've just decided to dive into the world of ChatGPT, and now you're eager to get started without feeling like you're deciphering hieroglyphics. Fear not; setting up ChatGPT is as straightforward as making a cup of tea—just a few steps, and you're ready to go. Begin by heading to the ChatGPT website, where you'll be greeted with a friendly sign-up page. Here, you can create an account using your email address or, if you feel fancy, with a quick sign-on option like Google or Microsoft. Once you've entered your email, crafted a strong password (something more creative than "password123"), and agreed to the terms, you'll receive a confirmation email. Click that link, and voilà, you're in! It's like being handed the keys to a brand new car, ready to explore the open road of AI possibilities.

Next, let's talk about the software installation. Thankfully, this isn't like putting together flat-pack furniture—no missing screws or confusing instructions. Simply follow the prompts on the screen to install the ChatGPT software on your device. It's akin to downloading your favorite app, straightforward and painless. Once installed, you'll find the ChatGPT icon waiting patiently on your desktop or app menu. Give it a click, and you'll be greeted by the interface as welcoming as your favorite cozy chair (dog hair excluded).

Now, onto the initial configuration. This step is where you personalize ChatGPT to suit your needs, like setting up a new smartphone. You can adjust settings to tailor the experience, choosing preferences that align with how you plan to use ChatGPT. Whether selecting themes for a personal touch or configuring notifications to keep you in the loop, these settings are designed to make your interaction a breeze. There's no need to call in the grandkids for help; the process is intuitive and user-friendly, just like chatting with an old friend.

SETTING UP CHATGPT:
A STEP-BY-STEP VISUAL GUIDE

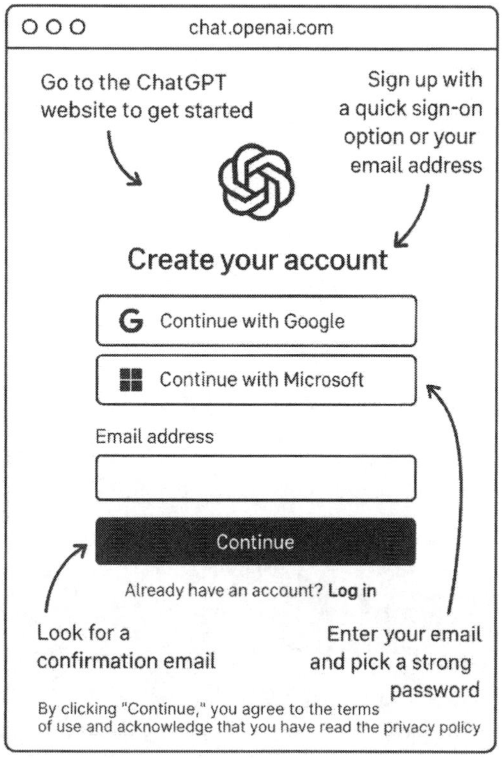

Let's address the hiccups you might encounter along the way. Nowadays, technology likes to test our patience with error messages. But worry not; these are usually as harmless as a squeaky floorboard. Common issues include connectivity glitches or login troubles. If the Wi-Fi decides to take a nap, a simple router reset often does the trick. For login woes, double-checking your email and password can save the day. And if all else fails, the trusty "Forgot Password" button is your ally. Remember, every problem has a solution, much like every puzzle has its missing piece.

In the spirit of getting hands-on, I encourage you to explore and experiment with ChatGPT's features. Think of it as a new playground where you can try different swings and slides. Start by typing simple prompts and see how ChatGPT responds. Ask it to tell you a joke, suggest a recipe, or plan a day trip. The more you engage, the more familiar and confident you'll become. Just like learning to ride a bike, it's a bit wobbly at first, but soon enough, you'll be cruising quickly.

So there you have it; the setup process is demystified and ready for you to tackle. With a bit of curiosity and a dash of enthusiasm, you'll be navigating ChatGPT like a seasoned pro in no time. Now, explore this digital realm, knowing you've got all the tools you need right at your fingertips.

Exploring ChatGPT's Key Features

Picture this: you've just settled into your favorite armchair with a cup of tea, ready to explore the wonders of ChatGPT. This AI marvel isn't just a one-trick pony; it boasts many features that can enhance your day-to-day life in ways you might not have imagined. At the heart of ChatGPT is its text generation capability. This means it can help you craft anything from a witty birthday card to a heartfelt letter, all with a few keystrokes from you. Imagine drafting this year's holiday newsletter, where you can effortlessly recount your family's latest adventures, sprinkle in some humor, and wrap it all up with a festive bow. No more staring at a blank page, wondering what to say. ChatGPT is there, ready to transform your thoughts into beautifully crafted prose.

Another standout feature is language translation. Remember when you tried to order a coffee in Paris and ended up with a croissant instead? Those days are over. With ChatGPT, you can practice your French, Spanish, or any other language, ensuring that your next café visit will result in the correct order. It's like having a personal language tutor who never asks for a day off. ChatGPT can help translate menu signs or even help you converse with the locals if you plan a trip abroad. Who knew impressing your travel companions could be as easy as having the right AI tool at your fingertips?

If you're anything like me, juggling appointments, family gatherings, and personal projects can sometimes feel like managing a three-ring circus. Here's where ChatGPT's scheduling assistant comes to the rescue. It can help organize your calendar, set reminders for important dates, and suggest the best time for your next family reunion based on everyone's availability. You'll have a new personal assistant who never forgets a birthday and always knows when the best sales are happening at your local mall.

Customization is key, and ChatGPT allows you to tailor its settings to fit your unique needs. Maybe you prefer responses with a touch of humor, or perhaps you want to focus on learning a specific language. Whatever your preference, ChatGPT can be adjusted to meet your requirements. Dive into the settings and make it your own, ensuring every interaction feels personal and relevant. It's similar to adjusting the seat and mirrors in a new car – once everything's set just right, the ride is smooth and enjoyable.

Now, I encourage you to let curiosity lead the way. Experiment with different features, try out new tasks, and see where ChatGPT can take you. Treat it like a new gadget you've just unwrapped, full of potential and excitement. Whether it's drafting a speech for a community event or finding the perfect pun for your next card game night, ChatGPT is ready to assist. And don't hesitate to share feedback or questions; this interaction helps refine the experience and make it even more helpful for everyone. So, go ahead, explore the possibilities, and enjoy the delightful surprises ChatGPT has in store.

Navigating the Interface: Understanding the Dashboard

Ah, the dashboard, your new digital command center! Imagine stepping into the cockpit of a sleek spaceship. Still, instead of buttons and levers that look like they belong in a sci-fi movie, you're greeted by a user-friendly interface that welcomes you with open arms. The ChatGPT dashboard is designed to be intuitive, with a layout that makes finding everything you need as easy as pie. As you open it, you'll see a menu on the left side, your go-to place for navigating different sections. This menu is like a well-organized spice rack, with everything labeled and within reach. You'll find options like "Home," "History," and "Settings," each leading you to a treasure trove of features. Above, you'll notice toolbars adorned with icons – tiny symbols that open the door to functionalities you'll soon come to love.

Now, let's talk navigation—think of it as learning to dance, where a few basic steps can take you a long way. The shortcut keys are your backstage passes, letting you switch between tasks without missing a beat. For instance, Ctrl + H might take you to your history, while Ctrl + S might save a conversation. These shortcuts are like the secret handshake among tech users, making your experience smoother and more efficient. And if you ever find yourself a bit lost, remember to follow the breadcrumbs at the top of the page. These little links help you track where you are and how you got there, much like the trail of popcorn you might have left during a family movie night.

Knowing what to prioritize is key to essential tools and sections. The "Home" section is your dashboard's living room, where you'll start each session. You can jump into conversations, check updates, or chat about your day with the AI. Next, the "History" section is your archive, storing past interactions like a digital scrapbook. It's perfect for revisiting previous conversations or retrieving that clever turn of phrase you conjured up last week. Don't overlook the "Settings" section, where you can personalize your experience. Adjust themes, customize notifications, and ensure everything is tailored to your liking—it's like decorating a room to make it feel just right.

Let me reassure you that navigating this dashboard doesn't require a degree in computer science. With simplified instructions and plain language guides, you'll find yourself gliding through the interface with the ease of a seasoned navigator. It's designed to be accessible, so you won't need to consult a tech dictionary whenever you want to change a setting. Think of it as following a well-marked trail in a familiar forest, where each step is clear and purposeful.

As you explore, you'll find that the ChatGPT dashboard becomes an extension of your digital life. It's a place where conversations flourish, ideas are born, and learning happens. Whether drafting a message to a lifelong friend or planning your next great adventure, the dashboard is your trusty companion, always ready to assist with a touch of humor and a wealth of knowledge. So, take a deep breath, dive in, and let the dashboard become your new favorite hangout spot in the digital world.

Troubleshooting Common Issues: Fear-Free Solutions

Ah, the joys of technology! It can make life wonderfully convenient, but let's face it, sometimes things go awry. Like that time, you tried to bake a soufflé and ended up with a pancake. No need to fret—troubleshooting ChatGPT isn't as daunting as it seems. Let's start with connectivity issues, which can feel like trying to tune an old radio. You know the drill: one minute, everything's fine, and the next, you're left staring at a spinning wheel of doom. Often, the culprit is a sleepy Wi-Fi connection that needs a little nudge. Restarting your router can work wonders, like shaking a ketchup bottle to get that last bit out. If that doesn't work, check if your device is connected to the correct network. Sometimes, it's the digital equivalent of trying to unlock your front door with a car key.

Then, there are misunderstood commands. Imagine asking your partner to pass the salt, only for them to hand you the pepper. ChatGPT can occasionally misinterpret prompts, and that's perfectly normal. Sometimes, it just needs a little clarity. If you find yourself in this pickle, try rephrasing your request. Be specific and clear, like asking for "two scoops of chocolate ice cream" rather than "something sweet." This helps ChatGPT understand precisely what you need, reducing the chance of it going rogue. And remember, patience is your friend here; technology can be a bit like a stubborn mule, requiring a gentle nudge in the right direction.

Fear not, for every problem has a solution, and here's a simple guide to keep your troubleshooting journey smooth. Begin with the basics: Is your device up to date? Software updates can be pesky, but they often solve unexpected glitches. Next, ensure that all cables and connections are secure. It's surprising how frequently the solution is merely a case of ensuring everything is plugged in properly. If you're still stuck, consider restarting your device. It's the tech equivalent of a good night's sleep – sometimes, it needs a little reset to function properly again.

Now, let's foster a problem-solving mindset. Picture yourself as a detective, piecing together clues. Approach issues with curiosity rather than frustration. Technology can be like a puzzle, and each piece you move brings you closer to solving it. Explore different solutions, and don't be afraid to experiment. After all, a little trial and error can lead to significant breakthroughs. Empower yourself with the knowledge that you have the tools to tackle these challenges, much like a seasoned gardener who knows that every weed can be uprooted with the right tool.

And, should you need a lifeline, numerous resources stand ready to assist. Online support forums brim with fellow users who've encountered similar issues and can offer tips or lend an empathetic ear. Much like gathering around a campfire to share stories, these communities are invaluable.

Additionally, don't hesitate to contact technical support if the problem persists. They're the cavalry, ready to charge in and save the day. Keep their contact information handy because even the best detectives sometimes need a little backup.

With these strategies in your toolkit, you'll find that technology's hiccups become less intimidating and more of an opportunity to flex your problem-solving muscles. So the next time ChatGPT seems to have gone on strike, take a deep breath, channel your inner sleuth, and dive into the mystery. Remember, every challenge is just an opportunity in disguise, waiting to be unraveled by your capable hands.

Reader Reviver Brain Break

This isn't a quiz. It's your café moment. Imagine this card waiting for you at a quiet table by the window, held gently in place by a beautiful marble pear. No rush – just a question served with curiosity.

Take a pause. Let your mind wander. And if an answer comes, scribble it in the margin, on a napkin, or whisper it into your coffee.

Sometimes, the long way is the best.

Practical Applications in Everyday Life

Imagine you're having a leisurely morning, sipping your coffee, and staring at your calendar, which resembles a jigsaw puzzle missing a few crucial pieces. Sound familiar? We've all been there, juggling appointments, errands, and social commitments while keeping our sanity intact. But what if I told you ChatGPT could be your personal assistant, ready to take on the chaos and turn it into a symphony of organized bliss? This little marvel of technology isn't just for tech enthusiasts; it's your new secret weapon to streamline planning and make your days run smoother than a perfectly brewed cup of tea.

Using ChatGPT for Daily Planning and Scheduling

Let's start by automating your calendar. Picture ChatGPT as a meticulous butler who never forgets a date. ChatGPT ensures you're always on schedule by syncing with your digital calendar, waving goodbye to those pesky double-bookings. It can suggest available appointment slots, making it feel like a game of Tetris where everything fits perfectly. Imagine setting up a lunch with your book club without the back-and-forth of emails or texts – ChatGPT handles the logistics, allowing you to focus on enjoying the conversation and maybe even squeezing in an extra chapter before the meeting.

And it doesn't stop there. ChatGPT is adept at setting reminders and gently nudging you about anniversaries, doctor appointments, or the yoga class you promised to attend. It's like having a friendly tap on the shoulder, ensuring nothing slips through the cracks. No more relying on sticky notes plastered across your fridge; ChatGPT keeps your reminders organized and timely, so you're always one step ahead.

Now, let's talk about task management. We all know the satisfaction of crossing off items on a to-do list, and ChatGPT takes this to a new level. It helps you prioritize tasks, ensuring you focus on what truly matters. ChatGPT becomes your productivity partner by generating daily to-do lists based on your priorities, nudging you to tackle that lingering chore or start that passion project. It's like having a motivational coach who knows your goals and cheers you every step of the way.

In the realm of productivity, time management is key, and ChatGPT offers practical tips to master this skill. Consider implementing time-blocking techniques, where you allocate specific time slots for tasks, creating a rhythm to your day that feels as harmonious as your favorite symphony. With ChatGPT suggesting the best times for focused work, breaks, and relaxation, you'll find yourself gliding through tasks with ease and efficiency.

Setting and tracking personal goals has never been easier. ChatGPT is your accountability buddy, guiding you on integrating SMART goals into your life—Specific, Measurable, Achievable, Relevant, and Time-bound. Whether you aim to learn a new language, write a novel, or simply start a new hobby, ChatGPT helps you break down your goals into manageable steps, track your progress, and celebrate your successes. It's like having a personal cheerleader, always encouraging you to reach for the stars.

Reflection Section

Consider jotting down one personal goal you want to achieve this month. Use ChatGPT to create a simple action plan with milestones and check in weekly to see your progress. Reflect on how ChatGPT's assistance has made the journey more manageable and rewarding.

ChatGPT is your digital ally, ready to transform how you organize and manage your daily life. It offers the tools to reduce stress and increase productivity, all with a touch of humor and empathy. Whether planning a family reunion, preparing for a new adventure, or simply trying to make the most of your day, ChatGPT supports and guides you every step. Now, go ahead and explore the wonders of organized living, where every day feels like a masterpiece waiting to be painted.

Recipe Discoveries: Culinary Adventures with ChatGPT

Imagine standing in your kitchen, apron on, ready to whip up a delightful meal. But instead of reaching for the same old cookbook, you have ChatGPT at your side. This isn't just any AI – it's your personal culinary guide, ready to whisk you away on a gastronomic adventure tailored to your tastes and needs. Whether you're catering to dietary restrictions or simply looking to spice things up, ChatGPT offers a treasure trove of recipe ideas. For those managing diabetes, it can suggest balanced meals that monitor sugar levels without sacrificing flavor. Think savory chicken dishes with roasted vegetables, ensuring you enjoy every bite without worry. Vegans, too, will find a friend in ChatGPT who can whip up plant-based delights like creamy mushroom risotto or spicy chickpea stir-fry. You'll have a new personal chef who understands your unique palate.

But ChatGPT's culinary prowess doesn't stop at individual recipes. It can help craft personalized meal plans that cater to your family's preferences and nutritional needs. Picture this: a week's worth of meals designed to satisfy every household member, from the picky eater to the adventurous foodie. ChatGPT can suggest a menu that balances proteins, carbs, and fats, ensuring everyone's dietary needs are met. Imagine starting the week with a hearty lentil soup and a mid-week treat of grilled salmon with quinoa salad. By the weekend, you'll be serving up a family favorite like homemade pizza with a twist – whole grain crust and a rainbow of veggie toppings. Its meal planning is made easy, with ChatGPT doing the heavy lifting so you can enjoy more time at the table with loved ones.

Not feeling confident in the kitchen? ChatGPT is here to help you level up your cooking skills with step-by-step guides that demystify even the most complex techniques. Ever wanted to perfect the art of searing a steak or baking the perfect loaf of bread? ChatGPT can guide you through each step, offering tips and tricks to ensure success. And if you're more of a visual learner, it can point you to video tutorials that show each move in action. You will thrive with this patient teacher by your side, encouraging you to try, learn, and savor the results. Before you know it, you'll serve dishes worthy of a family feast with newfound confidence and a dash of flair.

But why stop at familiar flavors? ChatGPT invites you to explore international cuisines, broadening your culinary horizons and bringing the world to your kitchen. Fancy an Italian night with homemade pasta and a rich tomato sauce? Or perhaps an Indian feast with aromatic spices transporting you to bustling markets? ChatGPT can suggest themes and dishes that make every dinner an adventure, from comforting classics to exotic new tastes. Imagine gathering your family for a Moroccan-inspired evening with fragrant tagine and couscous. Or hosting a Spanish tapas night, where each small plate offers a burst of flavor and a conversation starter. With ChatGPT, every meal becomes an opportunity to travel the globe, discovering cultures and tastes that inspire and delight.

So, as you stand in your kitchen, remember that ChatGPT is more than just a tool – it's your culinary companion, ready to inspire, guide, and celebrate each delicious moment. Whether you're a seasoned cook or just starting your culinary journey, ChatGPT makes every meal an adventure, one recipe at a time.

Streamlining Grocery Lists and Shopping with AI

It's Saturday morning, and you're about to brave the grocery store, determined to conquer the aisles with the precision of a well-oiled machine. But before setting foot outside, imagine having ChatGPT as your trusted shopping companion. This isn't just any AI; it's a savvy helper capable of generating grocery lists tailor-made for your household needs. By scanning your planned meals and existing pantry inventory, ChatGPT crafts a list that ensures you've got everything from the essentials to those little luxuries you love. It's as if you've got a culinary clairvoyant, predicting your needs with uncanny accuracy and ensuring you never run out of your favorite marmalade or that sneaky late-night snack.

Now, let's talk about finding deals—because who doesn't enjoy a good bargain hunt? ChatGPT can transform you into the Sherlock Holmes of shopping, armed with price comparison tools that reveal the best deals in town. Whether tracking down the elusive half-price chocolate or pinpointing a coupon for your preferred tea brand, ChatGPT's got your back. It can even suggest local promotions you might not have noticed, giving you the inside scoop on where to find the freshest produce at the best price. Imagine the satisfaction of filling your trolley knowing you've snagged the best deals, all without endlessly scrolling through flyers or fiddling with multiple apps.

As you prepare for your shopping trip, ChatGPT offers tips to organize your route efficiently, ensuring you glide through the store like a seasoned pro. It's like having a GPS for grocery shopping, optimizing your path to minimize time spent wandering aimlessly. By suggesting the best order for aisles and strategically plotting your course, you'll be in and out before you know it, with no forgotten items or unnecessary detours. You can even plan stops at nearby stores if there's a deal worth the extra mile, making your trip more than just a chore – it's a well-planned excursion.

And then there's the issue of waste – something we all want to reduce for our wallets and the planet. ChatGPT supports smart shopping practices, helping you buy what you need to avoid the dreaded fridge purge of wilted greens and expired yogurt. With portion control suggestions, ChatGPT ensures you're buying the right amounts, which is perfect for avoiding overstocking and underusing. It also tracks expiry dates, gently reminding you to use that carton of eggs before they're old enough to apply for a senior discount. Imagine a kitchen where everything you purchase has a purpose, each item used to its fullest potential before it's time to restock.

Interactive Grocery List Template

Create your own digital grocery list using a simple template. Include sections for pantry staples, fresh produce, and weekly specials. Use ChatGPT to customize this list, and try updating it before each shopping trip to keep it current and tailored to your needs.

So, as you prepare for your next shopping adventure, remember this: ChatGPT isn't just a tool; it's your grocery guru, ready to make every trip efficient, cost-effective, and environmentally friendly. It's like having a personal shopper who knows you better than you know yourself, ensuring your pantry is always stocked with the essentials and a few treats to make life a little sweeter. Whether planning a quiet dinner for two or a feast for the grandkids, ChatGPT helps bring order to your shopping chaos, leaving you more time to enjoy the things that truly matter.

Simplifying Household Chores with ChatGPT Assistance

Imagine standing in your living room, surveying the scene of a week's worth of life lived – with all its joyful chaos. Toys are scattered like confetti, and a mysterious stain has appeared on the carpet that you're sure wasn't there yesterday. It's the perfect time to call upon ChatGPT, your new ally in domestic bliss. Start by setting up customized cleaning schedules, transforming a daunting task into a manageable routine. ChatGPT can help you create weekly cleaning checklists, breaking down chores into bite-sized tasks that fit seamlessly into your schedule. It's like having a personal organizer who never gets tired or mutters under their breath about the state of the bathroom mirrors. And when spring cleaning season rolls around, it can suggest seasonal deep-cleaning plans, ensuring nothing gets overlooked, from the cobwebs in the seldom-used guest room to the garage that doubles as a time capsule of forgotten hobbies.

Now, let's move on to the DIY home maintenance tips because a bit of elbow grease goes a long way, and sometimes, the faucet drips louder than your grandkids during a game of hide and seek. ChatGPT offers practical advice for tackling simple repairs, guiding you through the process with the patience of a seasoned handyperson. Need to fix a leaky faucet? ChatGPT provides step-by-step instructions, ensuring you don't accidentally flood the kitchen in your quest for quiet. It can also help you establish lawn care schedules, transforming your garden into a verdant oasis that even your neighbor's begonias will envy. ChatGPT keeps your outdoor spaces looking their best, from mowing tips to reminders about when to fertilize, all without needing a horticulture degree.

Regarding enhancing home organization, ChatGPT is like a decluttering guru, gently nudging you towards a more orderly life. Whether it's your overcrowded kitchen cabinets or that hall closet that seems to defy the laws of physics, ChatGPT suggests strategies to streamline and simplify. It offers practical storage solutions, helping you make the most of your available space, even if that means finally letting go of that collection of novelty mugs from places you can barely remember visiting. With ChatGPT's guidance, every room in your house can become a sanctuary of calm, where everything has its place, and finding your keys doesn't involve a search party.

In supporting eco-friendly practices, ChatGPT acts as your green conscience, reminding you of the small changes that can significantly impact you. Recycling tips are just a question away, with ChatGPT advising on what goes where and ensuring nothing recyclable ends up in the wrong bin. It can also offer energy-saving ideas, like suggesting the best times to run your dishwasher or reducing your heating bill without knitting an extra layer of sweaters. Imagine the satisfaction of knowing your home is organized and kinder to the planet, thanks to a few simple adjustments guided by ChatGPT.

So, whether tackling a mountain of laundry or planning a weekend of home improvements, remember that ChatGPT is there to help you simplify and streamline. With its support, household chores become less of a burden and more of an opportunity to create a home that reflects your values and lifestyle. Imagine walking through your front door, greeted by a welcoming and serene space where every task is controlled, and every corner radiates warmth and order. That's the magic of combining technology with humor and empathy, transforming the everyday into something extraordinary.

Creating Personalized Reminders for Family Events

Picture this: you're sipping your morning coffee, and suddenly, it dawns on you – it's Aunt Edna's birthday tomorrow, and you've got nothing planned. No need to panic. ChatGPT is your trusty sidekick, ready to ensure you never miss another family occasion. Setting up event notifications is as simple as chatting with a friend. You tell ChatGPT about birthdays, anniversaries, or any special date, and it dutifully reminds you in advance. Imagine receiving a timely nudge to get that perfect gift for Uncle Joe or calling your cousin halfway across the world. With ChatGPT, you're always the star family member who never forgets to celebrate the ones you love.

Planning family gatherings can often feel like you're trying to organize a mini United Nations summit. Everyone has their preferences, and finding a suitable venue can be like searching for the Holy Grail. ChatGPT simplifies this by offering venue selection tips tailored to your needs, whether a cozy backyard barbecue or a grand celebration at a local hall. It can even help with guest list management, ensuring you don't accidentally leave out Great Aunt Mildred, who loves to remind everyone of the time you forgot her at the last reunion. With ChatGPT, coordinating these events becomes a breeze, allowing you to focus on the joy of bringing everyone together.

Once the venue is sorted, it's time to enhance communication. ChatGPT helps streamline conversations and keep everyone in the loop. You can effortlessly share updates using group messaging templates, ensuring everyone knows the plan. It's like having a digital megaphone broadcast your messages clearly and quickly. For those who prefer a more visual approach, setting up a shared calendar allows family members to see all upcoming events. Whether it's a casual brunch or a formal gathering, everyone stays informed and connected, eliminating those pesky moments of confusion or miscommunication.

Now, let's add a personal touch. ChatGPT isn't just about the significant events; it's also perfect for creating custom reminders for special occasions that hold meaning for your family. Perhaps you have a holiday tradition of baking Grandma's famous apple pie. ChatGPT can remind you to gather the ingredients in advance, ensuring no one misses out on nostalgia. Or maybe your family has a quirky tradition of watching cheesy holiday movies together—ChatGPT ensures you've got the popcorn ready and the streaming service queued up. These small reminders add a layer of thoughtfulness, making every occasion feel special and well-prepared.

Family life is filled with these meaningful moments, and with ChatGPT, you have a tool that ensures nothing slips through the cracks. It's more than just an AI; it's like a family calendar that remembers all the little things, ensuring you're always prepared for whatever comes your way. Whether it's a big celebration or a cherished tradition, ChatGPT helps you keep the spirit of family alive, one reminder at a time.

Managing Travel Itineraries with ChatGPT

Picture this: you've finally decided to take that long-awaited trip, perhaps a scenic drive along the coast or exploring the hidden gems of a foreign city. Excitement is in the air, but so is the looming task of planning. Enter ChatGPT, your trusty travel companion, ready to whisk away the stress and transform trip planning into a delightful experience. Start using ChatGPT's destination research tools to uncover your chosen location's must-see spots and local secrets. Whether it's the best cafés for people-watching or the historical sites that tell the story of a place, ChatGPT can help you create a travel timeline that caters to your interests. Imagine having a detailed itinerary that balances sightseeing with relaxation, ensuring you get the most out of your adventure without feeling rushed.

Now that your itinerary is shaping up, it's time to handle accommodations and activities. ChatGPT is like a savvy travel agent, guiding you to find the perfect places to stay. Whether you prefer the comfort of a cozy bed and breakfast or the luxury of a five-star hotel, ChatGPT can suggest options that fit your budget and preferences. It also has a knack for uncovering unique activities that elevate your travel experience, from guided tours to local workshops. Perhaps you'd enjoy a cooking class with a local chef or an evening river cruise to soak in the city lights. Booking these experiences through ChatGPT ensures you're not just a tourist but an active participant in the life and culture of your destination.

As you prepare for departure, keeping track of travel documents becomes paramount. ChatGPT steps in like a meticulous organizer, reminding you of passport and visa requirements well in advance. It suggests storing digital copies of essential documents in a secure location. Hence, you have peace of mind knowing everything is at your fingertips. No more last-minute scrambles to find your boarding pass or hotel confirmation – ChatGPT keeps you organized and ready to go, freeing you to focus on the anticipation of new experiences.

Of course, travel plans rarely go off without a hitch. That's where ChatGPT truly shines, adapting to changes with agility and ease. Imagine you've planned a day at the beach, only to wake up to rain clouds. Rather than letting the weather dampen your spirits, ChatGPT can suggest alternative activities, like a visit to a nearby museum or an indoor market. It also helps you seize spontaneous opportunities, perhaps recommending an impromptu visit to a local festival you hadn't heard about. With ChatGPT, you're always equipped to make the best of every situation, turning potential setbacks into new adventures.

So, as you embark on your next journey, remember that ChatGPT is more than just a planning tool – it's your partner in exploration, ready to enhance every aspect of your travel experience. Whether navigating bustling city streets or relaxing in a quiet village, ChatGPT ensures every moment is memorable, filled with the joy of discovery and the comfort of knowing you have a trusty guide. As you set off on your travels, savor each new sight, sound, and taste, knowing that with ChatGPT, the world is truly at your fingertips, waiting to be explored.

Reader Reviver Brain Break

Here's your moment to pause – with a question as quirky as the ladybug rock holding it up.

Not every decision has to be profound. Not every use of AI has to be practical.Sometimes, it's fun to wonder about the what-ifs, the maybes, the I-don't-knows.

Would you hand over your washing basket to a digital helper? Or are there things you still like to do the long way... just because?

Let yourself meander. There's no correct answer here. Just a question. A smile. And maybe a fresh pair of folded socks.

Bridging Generational Gaps

Have you ever sat across from your grandchild at a family gathering, wondering what magical language they speak? Fear not! You're not alone in navigating the intriguing world of emojis, memes, and TikTok dances. I once had a delightful conversation with my granddaughter, who was passionately explaining her latest school project. She used terms like "TikTok viral" and "FYP," and I nodded as if I knew exactly what she was talking about. At that moment, I realized the importance of bridging our generational gap. Enter ChatGPT, which can help turn those moments of bewilderment into engaging conversations that make you the cool grandparent in the know.

When it comes to crafting engaging conversations with your grandchildren, ChatGPT is like a treasure trove of conversation starters. Imagine asking your grandchild about their school project and receiving more than a one-word reply. With ChatGPT, you can generate prompts that pique their curiosity and spark meaningful discussions. Whether delving into their latest science experiment or exploring their favorite sports, ChatGPT provides ideas encouraging them to open up. You might ask, "What's the coolest thing you learned in school this week?" or "Tell me about the game you played at recess!" These prompts show your interest and make them feel valued, turning every chat into a memorable experience.

Of course, effective communication is a two-way street. ChatGPT can also help you enhance your communication skills, ensuring you're hearing and genuinely listening. Active listening exercises guide you to focus on your grandchild's words, making them feel heard and understood. Using empathy-building prompts, you can respond with warmth and understanding, creating a safe space for them to share their thoughts. Picture yourself saying, "That sounds fascinating! How did it make you feel?" It's these little touches that transform ordinary conversations into extraordinary connections.

Let's not forget the power of interactive dialogues. ChatGPT can simulate role-playing scenarios, allowing you to practice conversations before they happen. Whether preparing to discuss a sensitive topic or simply wanting to share a fun story, these simulations make you feel more confident and prepared. Imagine stepping into a world of story-based conversation starters, where you and your grandchild create tales of adventure and imagination. It's like having a mini-theater in your living room, where every dialogue is a new act in your shared play.

Incorporating technology comfortably is another way to bridge the generational gap, and ChatGPT is here to guide you through it. Text messaging is often the preferred method of communication for younger generations, and with ChatGPT's help, you can master the art of texting etiquette. Learn when to use emojis, how to interpret abbreviations, and what to do when they send you a meme that leaves you puzzled. You'll soon be quickly exchanging messages, feeling like a pro fluent in digital lingo.

Social media platforms can also be daunting, but with ChatGPT's guidance, you can navigate them like a seasoned explorer. Whether understanding the basics of Instagram or knowing how to comment on a Facebook post, ChatGPT provides insights that make you feel at home in the digital world. Picture yourself sharing a post that elicits a flurry of likes and comments from family and friends, boosting your social media confidence.

Reflection Section

Take a moment to reflect on a recent conversation with your grandchild. What went well, and what could be improved?

Use ChatGPT to generate a few new conversation starters and practice them before your next chat.

Bridging generational gaps is not just about understanding; it's about connection. With ChatGPT by your side, you're equipped to embark on this exciting journey, transforming every interaction into an opportunity for growth and joy. Through thoughtful conversations, active listening, or mastering technology, you're building a bridge that brings you closer to the ones you love. So, the next time you sit down with your grandchild, remember that you're not just having a conversation but creating a lasting bond that transcends generations.

Planning Intergenerational Activities with AI

Let's imagine a lively Saturday afternoon where the whole family gathers for fun and learning, from the youngest to the wise elders. You want to make sure everyone from the toddlers to the teens – and yes, even the adults – has a grand time. Here's where ChatGPT steps in like a trusty sidekick. You can use it to brainstorm many activities that offer something for everyone. Maybe it suggests a DIY craft project where you make bird feeders using recycled materials around the house. It's an excellent way to teach the young ones about sustainability while getting a little crafty. Or perhaps ChatGPT proposes a simple science experiment, turning your kitchen into a mini-lab equipped with baking soda volcanoes or homemade slime. These activities aren't just fun; they spark curiosity and learning across generations, creating memories that'll be discussed for years.

Once you've selected the perfect activities, the next task is coordinating the planning efforts. Picture this: ChatGPT as your event planner, organizing everything from start to finish. It can help you set a timeline for your family day, ensuring everyone knows when and where to be. No more last-minute chaos or forgotten supplies! ChatGPT can generate a resource list detailing all the necessary items, from glue sticks to safety goggles. You'll have a digital checklist, ensuring you're as prepared as a scout troop on a camping trip. This level of organization means you can focus on enjoying the event instead of worrying about missing pieces, creating a seamless experience for all involved.

Now, ensuring everyone participates can sometimes feel like herding cats, especially when there's a wide age range. But fear not! ChatGPT lends a hand by crafting inclusive game rules that cater to all skill levels and interests. It suggests ways to adapt activities, ensuring that even the littlest ones can join without feeling left out. For instance, if you're playing a game of charades, ChatGPT might propose using picture cards for the younger kids while the older ones act out more complex scenes. It also offers participation encouragement techniques, like assigning team roles to each person's strengths. This way, everyone's engaged, and no one feels like they're just watching from the sidelines.

After a day filled with laughter and learning, reflecting on shared experiences can enhance the moment's joy. ChatGPT can guide you through post-activity discussions, offering group discussion prompts and encouraging everyone to share their thoughts and feelings. You might ask, “What was your favorite part of the day?” or “What new thing did you learn?”. These questions open the floor for heartfelt exchanges and build a sense of community. Additionally, ChatGPT can suggest memory-sharing exercises, like creating a scrapbook that captures the highlights of the day. This allows everyone to contribute perspective, tangibly preserving the day's magic.

So, picture yourself surrounded by family, the room buzzing with excitement, and the smell of freshly baked cookies wafting through the air. Thanks to ChatGPT, you've got a plan that entertains and educates you. It’s more than just a day of activities; it’s an opportunity to connect, learn, and grow together. And as you pack up the supplies and bid farewell, you know this isn’t just an afternoon well-spent—it's another chapter in the beautiful tapestry of family life, woven with care and a little help from technology.

Using ChatGPT for Family Storytelling and Memory Sharing

Imagine sitting around the dinner table, stories weaving through the air like a tapestry of family lore. These tales are the threads that connect generations, each one adding a new hue to the family's rich narrative. But how often do these precious stories get lost in the hustle of everyday life, only to be recalled in snippets at family gatherings? This is where ChatGPT comes in; your digital scribe is ready to capture these moments and preserve them for posterity. Start by gathering family stories, and think of ChatGPT as the friendly interviewer, always prepared with a question that draws out the gems. It might suggest asking, "What was the most adventurous thing you did as a teenager?" or "Tell me about a time when you felt proud of your family." These questions are designed to open the floodgates of memory, encouraging detailed responses that paint a vivid picture of past events.

Once the stories start flowing, you might wonder how to structure these memories into a coherent narrative. ChatGPT excels here, too, offering templates to help you stitch individual anecdotes into a seamless tapestry. Whether it's structuring a story around a central theme or creating a timeline of family milestones, ChatGPT provides narrative-building techniques that transform raw memories into engaging tales. Imagine crafting a story that begins with your grandparents' immigration journey, weaving in tales of resilience, love, and adventure, leading to present-day family traditions. It's like assembling a puzzle where each piece clicks into place, revealing the bigger picture. This family narrative resonates with everyone who reads it.

Now, preserving these memories digitally ensures they withstand the test of time, and ChatGPT is the perfect tool for this task. Your digital archivist organizes stories, photos, and videos into a comprehensive collection. ChatGPT can suggest digital archiving solutions that keep everything neatly cataloged, from digitizing old photographs to tagging videos so they're easily searchable. Imagine having a digital family album accessible to everyone, where a simple search can bring up Aunt Mabel's legendary apple pie recipe or Grandpa's wartime letters. It's like having a family history library at your fingertips, ready to be explored by curious minds and future generations.

But why stop there? Sharing stories creatively brings new life into family memories, and ChatGPT offers many ideas. Picture turning a collection of stories into a multimedia presentation, with audio recordings of family members narrating their favorite tales. ChatGPT can assist in producing these audio stories, guiding you through recording, editing, and even adding sound effects for dramatic flair. Or perhaps you'd like to create an illustrated storybook, where each page comes alive with drawings that capture the essence of your family's adventures. ChatGPT can help you plan the layout, ensuring each illustration complements the text and creating a book that's as much a work of art as a keepsake.

These creative endeavors preserve family history and engage younger generations, making history tangible and exciting. Imagine grandkids gathered around, listening to a storybook that's not just any tale but their own family's saga, filled with heroes, humor, and heart. It's a way to pass down values, lessons, and love, ensuring that each new generation appreciates the legacy they inherit. So, as you embark on this storytelling adventure, remember that with ChatGPT, each story is not just a memory; it's a gift to the future.

Understanding Teen Slang: ChatGPT as a Cultural Bridge

You've undoubtedly been there: sitting at the dinner table, nodding as your teenage grandchild rattles off phrases that sound like an entirely new language. "Lit," "yeet," "sus" –

what do these even mean? Fear not, because understanding teen slang doesn't have to be an enigma wrapped in a conundrum. Think of ChatGPT as your personal interpreter, bridging the generational gap. It deciphers contemporary slang, providing you with not only the meanings but also examples of how these words fit into their chatty context. For instance, when your grandchild tells you something is "lit," ChatGPT will explain that this means exciting or excellent. And if they mention something sounds "sus," you'll understand they're questioning its legitimacy. It's like having a pocket guide to the ever-evolving teen lexicon, ensuring you're not left in the conversational dust.

But why should you bother with all this slang? Understanding these terms can significantly enhance communication and reduce all-too-common misunderstandings. When you grasp the slang, it's like speaking a bit of their language, showing that you care about their world. It's a small but mighty bridge over the generational divide. Imagine your grandchild's look of surprise and delight when you casually drop a perfectly timed "no cap" into a conversation. Suddenly, you're not just a grandparent – a relatable confidant, someone they can comfortably share with. This cross-generational understanding fosters closeness, turning casual chats into deeper connections.

Staying updated with these trends might seem daunting, but it doesn't have to be. ChatGPT offers trend analysis tools that keep you in the loop with the latest lingo and pop culture phenomena. Whether it's the latest viral meme or a new dance craze on TikTok, you'll be equipped to engage in conversations that might otherwise have seemed like foreign territory. By keeping up with these trends, you're not just learning a language but gaining insights into what shapes their world. This knowledge enriches your conversations, making them more meaningful and colorful.

Moreover, promoting language learning is an exciting way to keep your mind sharp and your conversations lively. ChatGPT can guide you through vocabulary expansion activities, introducing new words into your daily chatter. Why not make a game out of it? Challenge yourself to use a new slang term each week and see how your grandkids react. They might start looking forward to your following words, turning language learning into a delightful family tradition. It's an excellent exercise in adaptability and openness, which keep us young. Language practice sessions can also be a fun family activity, encouraging everyone to learn together. This shared experience becomes a bonding opportunity, reinforcing learning as a lifelong adventure.

With ChatGPT, you're not just a spectator of the evolving language landscape but an active participant. Embrace the slang, the trends, and the quirks of modern communication. It's a chance to relate, learn, and laugh alongside your loved ones. You'll find that with each new word and phrase, you're not only expanding your vocabulary but also expanding your world. And isn't that what life's all about?

Collaborating on Family Projects with ChatGPT

Imagine sitting around the kitchen table with your family, the air buzzing with ideas about a new project everyone wants to embark on together. It could be as simple as creating a family photo album or as ambitious as starting a community garden. But where to start? This is where ChatGPT plays the role of an innovative project manager, ready to help you launch collaborative family projects that foster teamwork and creativity. Picture this: family brainstorming sessions where everyone throws ideas into the ring, each more imaginative than the last. ChatGPT can offer project brainstorming sessions that help structure these ideas, ensuring no brilliant thought gets left behind. Perhaps you're interested in a project that combines everyone's love for cooking and storytelling, leading to a family cookbook filled with cherished recipes and tales from the kitchen. With ChatGPT, you can transform these sessions into a treasure trove of creativity, turning dreams into actionable plans.

Once the project is underway, managing tasks efficiently becomes the next hurdle. Enter ChatGPT, your organizational ally. Imagine it as a digital Swiss Army knife, helping you keep track of project progress with tools like Gantt charts and milestone tracking. These tools are invaluable in breaking the project into manageable tasks, assigning responsibilities to each family member, and setting deadlines that keep everyone accountable. Whether it's Dad handling the photography, Grandma writing down her secret pie recipe, or the kids designing the layout, ChatGPT ensures that every piece of the puzzle fits perfectly. It will be like having a conductor for your family orchestra, ensuring everyone hits the right notes at the right time.

Projects are a fantastic way to encourage each family member to contribute their unique skills and talents. ChatGPT sparks creativity by providing brainstorming prompts that inspire each person to bring their best. Perhaps your nephew has a knack for graphic design, while your sister is a whiz with words. ChatGPT can help identify these strengths, suggesting skill-sharing opportunities that allow everyone to learn from each other. Imagine the joy of seeing a project come together, each person playing a pivotal role, and the pride of contributing to something meaningful. It's more than just a project; it celebrates family unity and collaboration.

And speaking of celebrations, once the project is complete, it's time to acknowledge the hard work and dedication that went into it. ChatGPT is here to help you plan the perfect celebration, whether a small family gathering or a grand event. It can offer tips for planning a celebration that reflects the project's spirit, complete with decorations, food, and activities that bring the theme to life. Imagine a day filled with laughter, clinking glasses, and heartfelt speeches. ChatGPT can even suggest templates for acknowledgment speeches, ensuring you capture the essence of gratitude and appreciation for each family member's contribution. Picture standing in front of your family, with a smile on your face and a glass raised high, as you thank each person for their part in making the project a resounding success.

Ultimately, it's not just about the project but the journey of collaboration, creativity, and connection. With ChatGPT by your side, family projects become more than tasks to complete; they're experiences to cherish. Each project is an opportunity to learn, grow, and celebrate together, strengthening the bonds that make family life rich and rewarding. So, gather around the table, bring your ideas, and let ChatGPT help turn them into something extraordinary.

Developing Family Games and Quizzes

Imagine a rainy afternoon when you're all huddled indoors, looking for something to stave off the dreaded phrase, "I'm bored!" This is where creating custom family games with ChatGPT becomes your secret weapon. Picture yourself designing a trivia game tailored to your family's quirks and interests. You can craft questions that test knowledge about family history, favorite vacation spots, or even your family's legendary dessert recipes. ChatGPT can suggest topics and questions, making trivia night as exciting as the last family reunion when Grandpa unveiled his dance moves. Or perhaps your family enjoys a good puzzle? ChatGPT can offer puzzle design tips, helping you create crosswords or word searches that are challenging and filled with inside jokes and family lore. It's weaving a tapestry of fun, one question or puzzle piece at a time, creating moments everyone will remember.

Incorporating educational elements into these games makes them fun. It adds a dash of learning, keeping minds sharp without anyone realizing they're learning. ChatGPT can help you develop educational quizzes that blend fun with knowledge, like a history quiz crafted around the family's ancestry or world events that happened during the lives of the family's elders. Imagine a board game that takes players on a journey through history, from when your grandparents were born to today, including fun facts about what was happening in the world at each stage. It's a fantastic way to teach and learn while playing, ensuring that every dice roll leads to discovery and laughter.

Games are also a splendid way to promote teamwork and collaboration. With ChatGPT's help, you can develop games that require players to work together towards a common goal. Think of a treasure hunt where clues are scattered around the house or garden, each leading to the next, and requiring family members to combine their skills. ChatGPT can suggest cooperative play strategies, ensuring that everyone has a role to play, from the smallest clue-finder to the mastermind who deciphers the final riddle. This strengthens bonds and teaches valuable teamwork skills, making every game a lesson in collaboration and fun.

Of course, the magic lies in ensuring these games are inclusive and accessible to all ages. With ChatGPT, you can adapt games to suit everyone, from toddlers to septuagenarians, ensuring no one feels left out. Consider modifying traditional games with age-appropriate rules or creating multi-generational game rules that allow everyone to participate at their level. Perhaps a game of charades with more straightforward clues for the little ones while the older kids take on more complex tasks. It's like orchestrating a symphony where each instrument plays its part, creating harmony and joy for all involved.

As you engage in these playful endeavors, you're doing more than just filling time; you're nurturing connections and creating a treasure trove of memories. With ChatGPT, the possibilities are endless, and the fun is just beginning. Games and quizzes become more than entertainment; they are the threads that weave the fabric of family life, colorful and rich with shared experiences. Let these games be the backdrop for laughter, learning, and love, whether it's a quiet evening or a lively gathering.

As we conclude this chapter, remember that bridging generational gaps is as much about shared experiences as understanding. Whether through stories, games, or projects, these activities draw us closer, one laugh and lesson at a time. As we turn the page, we'll explore how technology can enhance travel experiences, ensuring that every journey is as enriching as the time spent at home with family.

Reader Reviver Brain Break

Here's your gentle mental tide pool – anchored by a piece of driftwood, worn soft by time and tides.

Take a pause. Not everything needs to be efficient. Some things are meant to be simple and delightful – those moments help technology feel like a friend, not a machine.

Maybe it's the "ping" of a message from someone you love. Maybe it's the way your smart speaker mispronounces your dog's name. Maybe it's this very card, quietly waiting for your smile.

Let yourself drift with the question. No destination is needed.

Enhancing Travel Experiences

Picture the open road stretching before you, the promise of adventure in the air, and a trusty thermos of coffee within arm's reach. Ah, the joy of a road trip! There's something magical about the freedom to explore at your own pace, stopping wherever the heart desires. But let's be honest; planning the perfect road trip can feel like assembling a jigsaw puzzle with a few pieces missing. Fear not, dear traveler, for ChatGPT is your co-pilot, ready to transform your travel dreams into reality, ensuring you don't leave home without a plan – or your toothbrush.

When creating a custom itinerary, ChatGPT is like a seasoned travel agent with a knack for personalization. Say you're yearning to explore the scenic byways of the Great Ocean Road. Simply input your interests, such as must-see coastal views or charming small towns, and watch as ChatGPT crafts an itinerary that ticks all your boxes. It even considers your penchant for historical sites, suggesting stops at iconic lighthouses that have stood the test of time. This tool takes the guesswork out of route planning, letting you focus on the fun stuff – like deciding which snacks to pack or what playlist to blast.

But what's a road trip without a few delightful detours? ChatGPT excels at optimizing travel routes, ensuring you spend less time stuck in traffic and more time soaking in the scenery. It can help you avoid pesky construction zones and suggest scenic detours that lead to hidden gems. Imagine veering off the beaten path to discover a quaint village or a breathtaking vista that wasn't in the guidebook. These serendipitous moments make for the best stories, and ChatGPT makes you more likely to find them.

Now, let's talk about packing. If you're like me, forgetting something essential haunts your dreams. Enter ChatGPT, your digital packing assistant. It can generate packing lists tailored to your destination, weather, and planned activities. From road trip essentials like sunscreen and sunglasses to emergency supplies like a first-aid kit and a spare tire, ChatGPT ensures you're prepared for anything the road throws. No more frantic searches for that elusive phone charger or realizing you left your favorite hat behind.

Safety and comfort are paramount on any journey. ChatGPT is here to help you find rest stops and accommodations that cater to your needs. Whether traveling with a furry friend or requiring accessible facilities, ChatGPT can suggest pet-friendly lodging options and rest areas with all the amenities. Picture pulling into a charming B&B that welcomes both you and your four-legged companion with open arms – or a rest stop that boasts clean facilities and a beautiful picnic area, perfect for stretching your legs and enjoying a leisurely lunch.

Essential Road Trip Packing Checklist

Before your next road trip, use this checklist to organize your essentials. Add your own items with ChatGPT's help and print them out or save them on your phone for easy access on the go.

With these tips and tricks, you're well on your way to planning a smooth road trip like your favorite playlist. So, buckle up and let ChatGPT guide you on an unforgettable adventure where every mile brings new discoveries. Every stop is a chance to create cherished memories.

Discovering Local Attractions and Hidden Gems

Imagine this: you've arrived in a charming town, suitcase in hand, ready to explore beyond the usual tourist traps. Instead of joining the throngs of visitors at the heavily photographed spots, you're yearning for something more authentic-places where the locals gather and the stories run deep. Enter ChatGPT, your digital compass for uncovering hidden gems and unique attractions that offer a genuine taste of local life. Perhaps it leads you to a historical landmark tucked away from the bustling streets, where the past whispers through the walls, telling tales of yesteryears. Or maybe it points you to a lively artisan market with crafts that speak of the community's heart and soul. These discoveries don't just fill your itinerary; they enrich your experience, giving you a deeper connection to the place you're visiting.

With ChatGPT’s help, you can curate sightseeing tours tailored to your specific interests, creating a travel experience that feels as personal as a handwritten letter. Are you passionate about art and culture? ChatGPT can suggest galleries and exhibits that align with your tastes, offering a feast for the eyes and food for thought. And for those who prefer the great outdoors, it can map out nature and wildlife excursions that take you off the beaten path. Imagine wandering through a serene forest trail or spotting rare birds along a tranquil riverbank. These personalized tours allow you to explore at your own pace, savoring each moment as it unfolds. You’ll feel like you have a knowledgeable friend who knows all the best spots and is eager to share them.

Now, let’s talk about cultural events. Picture your trip coinciding with a vibrant local festival full of music, dance, and delicious street food wafting through the air. With ChatGPT, you won't miss out on these lively celebrations. It helps you identify local music festivals, traditional fairs, and parades that unite communities. These events offer a window into the local culture, where you can tap your feet to the beat of a drum circle or watch a parade float pass by, adorned with colors and creativity. Each event is a chance to join the festivities, laugh and dance with locals, and perhaps even learn a new folk dance step.

Beyond the sights and sounds, engaging with local communities can transform your travel experience from a simple visit to a meaningful exchange. ChatGPT can guide you to community events and volunteer opportunities, letting you give back to the places you visit. Imagine spending a morning helping out at a community garden or participating in a neighborhood cleanup. These acts of kindness leave a positive impact and allow you to meet locals, hear their stories, and share yours. It's a beautiful way to connect, understand, and feel like a part of the community, even briefly.

These unique attractions, tailored tours, cultural events, and community engagements transform travel from snapshots into a tapestry of experiences. With ChatGPT as your guide, you're not just visiting new places; you're immersing yourself in them, discovering the heart and soul of each destination.

Language Translation on the Go: Communicating Abroad

What if you were standing in a bustling market in the heart of a foreign city, surrounded by the vibrant colors and sounds of local life. You're eager to immerse yourself in the culture, but there's one slight hitch: the language barrier. Fear not, for ChatGPT is here to lend a hand, transforming you into a linguistic maestro. Begin using ChatGPT to learn basic phrases and vocabulary in the local lingo. Common travel expressions like "Where is the bathroom?" or "How much does this cost?" are at your fingertips, making those initial interactions a breeze. ChatGPT can also create language flashcards tailored to your needs, allowing you to practice on the go. Picture yourself impressing the locals with a well-timed "thank you" in their language, earning nods of appreciation and a warm smile in return.

But it doesn't stop there. When you're navigating unfamiliar menus or trying to ask for directions, ChatGPT provides real-time translation assistance. Imagine sitting at a cozy café, staring at a menu filled with culinary delights you can't quite decipher. With a quick input into ChatGPT, you receive instant translations, ensuring you order precisely what you crave without any surprises. Or perhaps you're trying to find your way to the nearest museum; ChatGPT can help you quickly ask for directions and understand the responses. These tools transform potential travel hiccups into seamless experiences, letting you focus on enjoying the journey rather than worrying about miscommunication.

Understanding a culture goes beyond words; it's about gestures, customs, and etiquette. ChatGPT can guide you through the cultural norms of your destination, ensuring you navigate interactions with grace and respect. Learn about greeting customs to know whether a handshake, a bow, or a friendly wave is appropriate. Dining etiquette tips ensure you don't accidentally offend your hosts, whether knowing not to tip in certain countries or understanding how to use chopsticks properly. These insights offer a deeper connection to the culture, showing your respect and willingness to learn from those around you.

Bridging communication gaps is more than just translating words; it's about fostering meaningful interactions. ChatGPT can provide multilingual conversation starters, allowing you to chat with locals and fellow travelers. Whether discussing the weather, local sports, or the best-hidden spots in town, these conversations open doors to new friendships and enriching experiences. Guided communication practice helps you feel more confident, turning hesitant attempts into fluid exchanges. Imagine sharing a laugh with a shopkeeper or exchanging travel tips with a fellow globetrotter, each interaction enriching your trip with stories and connections that transcend language.

ChatGPT becomes your travel companion as you explore new destinations, ensuring language barriers don't stand in the way of unforgettable experiences. It empowers you to connect, understand, and engage with the world around you in ways that leave you feeling like a true citizen of the globe. Whether ordering a meal, asking for advice, or simply greeting a stranger, these moments become the threads that weave your travel tapestry, vibrant and full of life.

Finding the Best Dining Options with AI Assistance

Imagine you're in a vibrant new city, your stomach rumbling after a day of exploring. The street is alive with the scent of sizzling delicacies and the chatter of locals. But where to eat? This is where ChatGPT steps in, like a culinary compass guiding you to the heart of the local food scene. Picture yourself wandering through narrow lanes, only to stumble upon a bustling street food stall that ChatGPT recommended. The flavors explode in your mouth, and you instantly feel like a local, savoring the authentic taste of the city. Or perhaps it leads you to a charming family-owned restaurant, where the owner greets you like an old friend and serves a dish that has been perfected over generations. These moments make travel unforgettable, and with ChatGPT, these experiences are just a prompt away.

Dietary preferences can often feel like a maze when you're away from home. ChatGPT can help you find dining options that cater to your needs, whether vegetarian, gluten-free, or picky eater. Imagine being in a foreign land, wondering if you'll have to settle for a salad again. Fear not! ChatGPT can point you to vegetarian-friendly venues that offer a smorgasbord of flavors, ensuring your meals are as exciting as they are nutritious. And for those avoiding gluten, ChatGPT can highlight places where the menu is as safe as it is delicious, so you can dine without worry. ChatGPT will be your personal dining assistant, knowing your preferences and always ready to offer a suggestion that hits the spot.

We've all experienced the frustration of arriving at a highly-rated restaurant only to find a line stretching around the block. This is where ChatGPT's savvy reservation skills come into play. Using online booking tools can help you secure a table at that must-visit eatery, allowing you to skip the wait and dive straight into a culinary adventure. Imagine walking past the queue, a knowing smile on your face, as you're ushered to your reserved table. It's a small yet satisfying victory, one that ChatGPT makes possible with just a few clicks.

But dining is more than just eating; it's an opportunity to explore and learn. ChatGPT encourages culinary exploration by guiding you to local cooking classes or food tours. Imagine donning an apron in a cozy kitchen and learning the secrets of traditional dishes from a local chef. It's more than just a class; it's a journey through culture and flavor, where every ingredient tells a story. Or perhaps you join a guided food tour, wandering from one delightful tasting spot to another, each bite revealing a new layer of the city's culinary identity. These experiences not only tantalize your taste buds but also enrich your understanding of the place you're visiting.

Dining abroad is a feast for the senses, a celebration of culture, and an adventure. With ChatGPT as your guide, each meal becomes a story waiting to be savored, a memory crafted with care and shared over a table filled with laughter and discovery. ChatGPT ensures that every dining experience is as rewarding as the journey, whether you're a seasoned epicure or a curious food lover.

Exploring Virtual Tours and Experiences

Picture yourself exploring the world's wonders, all from the comfort of your favorite armchair. With the magic of virtual reality, you can now stroll through the halls of the Louvre or gaze at the ancient ruins of Machu Picchu without the hassle of airport security. ChatGPT is your gateway to these immersive experiences, offering a wealth of virtual reality tours that transport you to famous landmarks and museums across the globe. Imagine donning a VR headset or simply using your computer to wander through the Smithsonian's exhibits, each artifact and display brought to life through future technology. Your personal tour guide will never tire of your questions and will provide insights and stories at every turn.

But why stop at museums? The world of virtual experiences extends far beyond, offering a rich tapestry of cultural events and performances that can be enjoyed from anywhere. ChatGPT can guide you to live-streamed theater performances, where the thrill of the stage comes alive before your eyes. Whether it's a Shakespearean classic or a modern play, these performances offer a front-row seat to creativity and art. And for music lovers, imagine attending a virtual concert where your favorite band plays their hits, the crowd's energy palpable even through a screen. These events aren't just entertainment; they're a way to feel connected to a global community, sharing the joy and passion that only live performances can bring.

Beyond the world of performance, virtual workshops offer a chance to learn and grow, adding new skills to your repertoire. ChatGPT can help you find online seminars that cater to your interests, from pottery making to digital photography. Picture yourself shaping clay into a beautiful vase, guided by a skilled artisan who shares tips and tricks over video. It's more than just a hobby; it's a doorway to creativity and expression, where each workshop is a chance to learn something new. These experiences enrich your life, offering a sense of accomplishment and pride in your creations. And who knows? You might even discover a hidden talent or a new passion that sparks joy.

In our interconnected world, fostering global connections has never been more accessible or rewarding. ChatGPT can introduce you to international discussion forums and cultural exchange groups where curiosity and camaraderie thrive. Imagine chatting with a pen pal from halfway across the world, sharing stories, traditions, and laughter. These forums become a bridge to understanding, where each conversation reveals the unique tapestry of cultures and perspectives. Engaging in these exchanges broadens your horizons and cultivates empathy and friendship, creating bonds that transcend borders and time zones.

These virtual tours and experiences offer a treasure trove of opportunities to explore, learn, and connect. With ChatGPT as your guide, the world is at your fingertips, ready to be discovered and enjoyed in innovative and inspiring ways. Whether through a VR headset or a lively online discussion, each experience is a chance to expand your understanding and appreciation of our diverse and wondrous world.

Curating a Travel Blog with ChatGPT

You've returned home from an exhilarating trip, your heart full of stories and your camera brimming with photos. Now, you're eager to share your adventures, not just with friends but with the world. Enter ChatGPT, your trusty sidekick in the world of blogging. It assists in drafting engaging travel stories by helping you structure your narrative like a seasoned storyteller. Think of it as having a literary buddy who nudges you to start with a captivating scene-maybe that unexpected encounter with a local artisan or the breathtaking sunrise you caught over a misty valley. ChatGPT suggests descriptive language that paints a vivid picture. It makes readers feel like they're with you, navigating a bustling bazaar or wandering through serene gardens. It's about drawing your audience into the scene, making them part of the story.

Visual storytelling adds an extra layer to your blog, and ChatGPT can guide you in incorporating visuals effectively. You might have a treasure trove of photos capturing the essence of your travels-each one a snapshot of a memory. ChatGPT can help you choose the best photos to complement your narrative, offering tips on composition and lighting that make your images pop. And let's not forget video content! Imagine integrating short clips of a lively street performance or the gentle lapping of waves against a sandy shore. When paired with your words, these videos create a multisensory experience for your readers, making your blog a delightful escape from the everyday grind.

Engagement is key to keeping your audience returning for more, and ChatGPT knows how to keep the conversation going. It suggests prompts for your readers to comment on, like asking them to share their own travel tips or favorite destinations. These interactions turn your blog into a community where stories and experiences are exchanged, and everyone feels part of a larger adventure. ChatGPT also provides strategies for sharing your posts on social media, ensuring your tales reach those eager for inspiration. Crafting catchy titles and intriguing snippets helps your blog stand out in the digital landscape.

Now, let's talk about turning your passion into profit. ChatGPT can suggest monetization options for your travel blog, opening doors to affiliate marketing partnerships and sponsored content opportunities. Picture collaborating with brands that align with your travel philosophy, whether eco-friendly gear or local tour companies. These partnerships support your blogging journey and offer value to your readers, providing them with insights and recommendations they trust. It's like having a trusted friend who knows the ins and outs of the travel industry, guiding you toward opportunities that fit your style.

Consistency is crucial in blogging, and ChatGPT can help you maintain a regular posting schedule. Assisting in setting up a content calendar ensures you have a clear plan, allowing you to focus on crafting quality content without the stress of last-minute scrambles. ChatGPT offers guidelines on posting frequency, helping you find a rhythm that works for you and your audience. It’s like having a personal assistant who keeps you on track, ensuring your blog remains an active and engaging space for readers to explore.

As we wrap up this chapter, remember that ChatGPT is here to support your blogging endeavors, whether crafting tales of far-off lands or sharing tips from your latest road trip. It's more than just a tool; it's a partner in creativity and connection. With your blog ready to captivate and inspire, let’s move on to the next chapter, exploring the exciting realm of safety and privacy in the digital age.

Reader Reviver Brain Break

Curiosity is powerful – but it can be tender, too. This little pine cone has been through wind, weather, and wilderness... and yet here it is, calmly holding space for your question.

Some searches are simple. Others feel a little too personal, a little too revealing.

But here, you don't need to hit "enter." Just wonder. Just whisper it. Or write it down if you dare.

No judgment. No cookies... Just you and your mind, roaming free.

Make A Difference

***** REVIEW

Every new skill begins with a single prompt – and your review could be the spark that encourages someone else to start their own journey.

When you share your thoughts, you're offering reassurance that whispers: "If they can do it, maybe I can too!"

Think of it as leaving a trail of coffee beans – or perhaps a plate of warm scones – so that fellow learners feel welcome to pull up a chair and join the ChatGPT Café.

By sharing your honest review, you help to:

- Inspire confidence in other beginners
- Keep the learning conversation alive and thriving
- Build a warm, supportive community of explorers

Thank you for being part of this journey. The real magic of ChatGPT isn't just in what it can do – it's in how we use it together, passing along discoveries like stories shared over a cozy cup of coffee.

Please leave your review on the platform where you found this book, or use this link:

[https://www.amazon.com/review/review-your-purchases/?asin=BOOKASIN]

With gratitude,
Margaret Fields

Lifelong Learning and Creativity

Imagine a blank page in front of you, a cup of tea by your side, and a world of stories waiting to be told. It's a scene ripe with possibility, where imagination knows no bounds and creativity leaps joyfully from one idea to another. This is the magic of writing – an adventure of the mind that anyone can embark on, regardless of age or experience. ChatGPT is ready to be your writing companion whether you've been penning poems since school or are just beginning to explore the written word. Picture it as your friendly muse, always eager to ignite your creativity with inspiration.

Let's delve into the art of engaging in creative writing prompts, a fantastic way to stimulate your imagination and unlock stories hidden within. ChatGPT offers a treasure trove of prompts to help you get started. Maybe you'll find yourself crafting a sci-fi tale about a distant galaxy where tea is the universal currency. Or perhaps you'll be drawn to a fantasy world where dragons deliver the mail. These prompts are designed to push the boundaries of your creativity and lead you down paths you never knew existed. But it doesn't stop at fiction; you can explore personal narratives, reflecting on your life experiences. Consider writing about a cherished memory from your childhood or a moment of triumph that still makes you smile. These exercises foster creativity and serve as a means of self-discovery and reflection.

Beyond sparking ideas, writing is a craft that can be honed and refined, much like a well-tended garden. ChatGPT is here to help you develop your writing skills, offering guidance on grammar and style. Think of it as your editor, gently nudging you toward more unambiguous sentences and compelling prose. Perhaps you're working on a short story and need feedback on plot development. ChatGPT can provide insights, suggesting ways to build tension or add depth to your characters. It's like having a seasoned writer at your fingertips, ready to offer a fresh perspective on your work.

To truly embrace writing, consider making it a daily practice. Writing can become a cherished routine, just as you might enjoy a morning walk or an evening game of cards. ChatGPT can provide daily journal prompts to kickstart your creativity, encouraging you to capture the small wonders of everyday life. You might write about the beauty of a sunrise, the joy of a shared meal, or the curiosity sparked by a new book. These prompts are exercises in writing and opportunities to slow down and savor the moment.

For those who enjoy a challenge, why not take on a writing challenge with ChatGPT's help? Set a goal to write a short story each week or explore a new genre every month. It's an exciting way to stretch your creative muscles and discover new facets of your writing style. Speaking of genres, the world of writing is vast and varied, offering endless possibilities for exploration. Dive into poetry, where words dance and emotions flow freely. Experiment with mystery, crafting intricate plots that keep readers on their seats. ChatGPT can provide exercises and outlines to guide your journey, ensuring you have the tools to succeed.

Interactive Element: Journaling Prompts for Creative Exploration

Consider trying out a few journaling prompts to inspire your writing...

Reflect on a favorite travel experience, capturing the sights, sounds, and feelings that made it memorable. Or write about a lesson learned from a cherished family tradition. These prompts encourage you to delve deeper into your experiences, uncovering stories that are uniquely yours.

As you explore the world of writing with ChatGPT, remember that creativity is more than just putting words on a page. It's about expressing yourself, connecting with others, and finding joy. So grab your pen, open your mind, and let the stories flow.

Solving Puzzles and Brain Teasers with ChatGPT

Picture this: it's a cozy afternoon, and you're settling into your favorite chair with a puzzle book. But instead of flipping through pages of pre-set puzzles, you're about to embark on a mental workout with ChatGPT as your guide. This clever AI can generate many brain teasers and puzzles, keeping your mind sharp and engaged. ChatGPT has something for everyone, whether you're a Sudoku enthusiast or a fan of logic riddles. Imagine tackling a Sudoku puzzle, where every number fits perfectly into its place, much like finding the last piece of a jigsaw. Or perhaps you'll prefer a logic riddle that challenges your reasoning skills, each answer leading to a satisfying "aha" moment. These exercises entertain and stimulate your brain, ensuring it's as active as a lively game of charades at a family gathering.

Engaging with puzzles is more than just fun – it's a fantastic way to develop problem-solving skills. As you work through various challenges, your critical thinking and analytical abilities sharpen like a knife on a whetstone. ChatGPT offers strategy tips to enhance your puzzle-solving prowess, guiding you through each step with patience and clarity. Whether it's advising you to start with the edges of a crossword or suggesting a systematic approach to a complex riddle, these insights transform potential frustration into triumph. Problem-solving exercises become a mental gym, where each completed puzzle is a small victory that builds your cognitive muscles. It's like training for a marathon but much easier on the knees.

Puzzles aren't just a solo endeavor-invite family and friends to join the fun, turning it into a collaborative adventure. ChatGPT can facilitate group puzzle activities, transforming your living room into a hub of excitement and camaraderie. Imagine organizing a virtual escape room scenario where everyone works together to solve clues and escape a digital conundrum. Or picture a group brain teaser challenge, where each member brings unique skills, creating a tapestry of teamwork and laughter. These sessions are perfect for fostering connection, as everyone contributes to the goal of triumphing over the challenge. It's a reminder that, much like in life, collaboration often leads to the most satisfying outcomes.

Tracking your progress and improvement is another key aspect of puzzle-solving with ChatGPT. The AI can help you monitor your cognitive abilities over time, offering insights into your development. ChatGPT acts as a personal trainer for your brain by scaling puzzle difficulty and assessing your skills. One day, you might find yourself breezing through puzzles that once seemed daunting, a testament to your growth and perseverance. Keeping track of your achievements not only motivates you to push further but also provides a sense of accomplishment that's incredibly rewarding. It's like having a report card, but you're earning badges of honor for your mental agility instead of grades.

Reflection Section

Take a moment to reflect on your puzzle-solving journey. What puzzles do you enjoy most, and how have they challenged you? Consider setting a goal to tackle a new puzzle each month, using ChatGPT's guidance to explore and expand your skills.

Document your progress and celebrate each milestone as a triumph of curiosity and persistence.

As you engage with puzzles and brain teasers, remember that each challenge is an opportunity to explore new ways of thinking, all while having fun. ChatGPT is here to make the experience enjoyable and enriching, ensuring that your mind stays as lively and vibrant as your spirit.

Exploring New Hobbies and Interests

It's a sunny morning, and you're standing in your backyard, hands caressing the earth, ready to plant the first seeds of your future garden. Gardening is not just about growing plants; it's about nurturing life and watching it flourish under your care. If you've ever felt the urge to turn your patch of grass into a lush oasis, look no further than ChatGPT for guidance. Whether you're a novice with a penchant for petunias or dreaming of a vegetable patch that rivals your neighbor's, ChatGPT offers tips tailored to your gardening aspirations. It can suggest which plants thrive in your climate, how to manage pesky pests, and even when to fertilize. Think of it as having a green-thumbed mentor in your pocket, ready to transform your backyard into a personal Eden.

Perhaps the allure of the skies captivates you more. Imagine stepping outside with binoculars embarking on a quiet birdwatching adventure. This relaxing hobby invites you to pause, observe, and marvel at the avian wonders fluttering by. ChatGPT can introduce you to this world, providing information on the best birdwatching spots and tips on identifying different species by their calls and colors. It's like having a knowledgeable birdwatching companion who doesn't mind being on call at all hours. Watching birds is a feast for the eyes and a balm for the soul, offering moments of tranquility and discovery.

Once a hobby piques your interest, diving deeper is where the fun begins. ChatGPT stands ready to assist in your quest for knowledge, guiding you to online forums filled with enthusiasts who share your passion. Whether it's photography tips shared by seasoned shutterbugs or craft ideas from a community of crafters, these forums are treasure troves of advice and camaraderie. Imagine joining a group of like-minded individuals, each at their own stage of the journey, eager to share insights and stories. ChatGPT can help you locate these communities and suggest resource guides and tutorials with step-by-step instructions to hone your skills.

As you dip your toes into these new interests, having beginner-friendly resources is invaluable. ChatGPT can point you to DIY craft tutorials that demystify complex projects, turning them into manageable and enjoyable activities. Whether you wish to create a colorful quilt or dabble in woodworking, these guides offer clear, concise instructions that make even the most ambitious projects achievable. For photography enthusiasts, ChatGPT can suggest beginner guides that cover everything from basic camera settings to composing your first breathtaking shot. Picture yourself capturing a sunset, each click of the shutter a step closer to mastering your newfound art.

Beyond personal enjoyment, hobbies flourish when shared. ChatGPT encourages collaboration by suggesting ways to connect with others. Joining hobby clubs can open doors to new friendships and shared experiences. Imagine attending a local gardening club meeting, where fellow gardeners swap seeds and stories, or participating in a photography workshop where you learn new techniques while capturing stunning vistas. For those who enjoy the comfort of home, hosting virtual hobby meetups is a delightful alternative. With ChatGPT's help, you can set up these gatherings, where everyone shares progress, tips, and a good laugh over video chat. These interactions enhance your skills and create a sense of belonging and community, turning solitary pursuits into shared adventures.

Learning a New Language with AI Assistance

Imagine sitting at your kitchen table, a cup of coffee steaming beside you, and embarking on a delightful linguistic adventure. Learning a new language can feel like unlocking a secret world where every word is a key to new experiences. With ChatGPT, this process becomes as enjoyable as discovering a new favorite book. Picture it as your friendly language tutor, armed with interactive exercises that make vocabulary learning feel like a game. You can create flashcards that whisk you away to different lands, each card revealing a new word to add to your growing arsenal. Imagine flipping through them, each turn of a card a step closer to fluency, like collecting treasures on a scavenger hunt. Regarding pronunciation, ChatGPT turns into a patient coach, guiding you through practice sessions with the precision of a seasoned conductor. You'll soon find yourself rolling those R's like a local, impressing everyone at the next family gathering.

Incorporating language practice into daily routines can transform learning from a chore into a delightful habit. Imagine starting your day with a quick chat with a language exchange partner halfway around the world, sharing stories over morning coffee. It's like having a pen pal but with the added bonus of speaking in a new tongue. ChatGPT can help you find these partners, creating opportunities for authentic conversations that deepen your understanding and appreciation of the language. And why not add a touch of creativity with bilingual storytelling activities? Gather your family for a storytelling session that switches between languages, weaving tales that captivate and educate. It's an experience that enhances language skills and brings everyone together in a shared adventure, making language learning a family affair.

Tracking your progress is crucial, and ChatGPT is there to help you quickly set and achieve language goals. Picture it as your personal coach, providing language proficiency assessments highlighting your strengths and improvement areas. It's like receiving a report card but without the anxiety-inducing red ink. With goal-setting templates, you can chart your progress, setting milestones that keep you motivated and on track. Maybe you aim to read a short story in your new language or talk about your favorite hobby by the month's end. Whatever your goals, ChatGPT helps you break them down into manageable steps, turning the learning process into a series of small victories. Each milestone reached is a reason to celebrate. Before you know it, you'll be chatting away with the confidence of a native speaker.

But learning a language is about more than words and grammar; it's a window into another culture. With ChatGPT, you can access cultural insights that enrich your understanding and make your learning experience genuinely immersive. Imagine exploring cultural etiquette guides that teach you the nuances of greetings, dining customs, and social norms. It's like having a cultural ambassador whispering tips in your ear, ensuring you navigate new social landscapes with ease and respect. ChatGPT can also guide you through discussions of historical context, providing a deeper appreciation for the language's evolution and the stories it tells. Picture yourself learning about the historical events that shaped the language you're studying, each fact adding a layer of richness to your understanding. It's a journey that turns language learning into a vibrant tapestry of cultural discovery, where every phrase and idiom carries the weight of history and tradition.

With ChatGPT as your guide, learning a new language becomes an enriching and enjoyable experience. It's a chance to connect with people from different backgrounds, explore new cultures, and expand your horizons. So grab your flashcards, warm up those vocal cords, and prepare to embark on a linguistic adventure that's as rewarding as fun.

Enhancing Artistic Skills with Creative Tools

You are sitting at your kitchen table. The morning sun casts a warm glow, and a blank digital canvas is in front of you. It's a world of endless possibilities, just waiting for a splash of creativity. Digital art platforms have revolutionized our expression, offering a playground where imagination takes center stage. With ChatGPT as your guide, you can explore these platforms, each a new adventure. Digital painting tutorials are a fantastic starting point for those who enjoy painting. Imagine the satisfaction of creating a masterpiece without the mess of brushes and paint pots scattered across the room. You can experiment with colors and textures with just a few clicks, creating landscapes that transport you to serene valleys or bustling cityscapes. And for those intrigued by graphic design, ChatGPT can introduce you to software guides that make design concepts accessible. From designing a simple family logo to crafting a digital scrapbook of cherished memories, these tools empower you to bring your artistic visions to life.

Art, much like life, is about exploration and play. It's about stepping outside your comfort zone and discovering new ways to express yourself. ChatGPT encourages you to experiment with various art styles and mediums, inviting you to try your hand at abstract art exercises. Picture yourself dabbling in bold, vibrant colors, creating shapes and patterns that evoke emotions and provoke thought. There's no right or wrong in abstract art, only the joy of personal expression. Mixed media projects offer another creative avenue, blending digital and traditional techniques. Imagine combining photography with digital painting, creating a unique piece that tells a story only you can tell. These projects are not just about the end result; they're about the journey of discovery, where each brush stroke or mouse click leads to a new revelation.

Feedback is a crucial part of any creative process, and ChatGPT is here to offer a constructive critique that helps you grow as an artist. Think of it as having a wise friend who gently points out areas for improvement while celebrating your strengths. Through composition analysis, ChatGPT can help you understand how to balance elements within your artwork, ensuring your pieces are visually harmonious. And when it comes to color theory, ChatGPT provides tips that transform your understanding of how colors interact, adding depth and vibrancy to your creations. Imagine the thrill of seeing your work evolve, each piece a little better than the last, each one a testament to your growth and dedication.

Art thrives in community, and connecting with fellow artists can be incredibly inspiring. ChatGPT can guide you to online art communities where you can share your work, receive feedback, and draw inspiration from others. Picture participating in online art exhibitions, where your digital masterpieces are displayed alongside those of artists worldwide. It's a chance to see your work through the eyes of others and appreciate the diversity and richness of perspectives that art brings. Artist collaboration projects are another exciting opportunity, allowing you to work with others to create something truly unique. Whether a joint digital painting or a group exhibition, these collaborations foster creativity, build friendships, and expand your artistic horizons.

With ChatGPT, enhancing your artistic skills becomes an exciting adventure filled with learning and growth. It's about finding joy in the process, embracing challenges, and celebrating achievements, big and small. Whether you're an experienced artist or just beginning to explore your creative side, a world of possibilities awaits you. So pick up your digital brush, let your creativity soar, and see where the journey takes you.

Discovering Online Classes and Workshops

Imagine settling into your favorite armchair, laptop in hand, ready to explore the vast world of online learning. It's a realm where curiosity knows no bounds, where every click opens the door to a new adventure. With ChatGPT by your side, finding and enrolling in online classes becomes as seamless as a Sunday morning stroll. Picture platforms like Coursera and Udemy, with courses catering to every interest, from photography to philosophy. Are you intrigued by learning a new skill, like graphic design or culinary arts? ChatGPT can guide you through specialized skill workshops that fit your personal learning goals. Whether you're seeking certification in a new field or simply wish to explore a hobby, these platforms offer a treasure trove of knowledge waiting to be discovered. Think of them as digital libraries, each course a new chapter in your lifelong learning story.

But why stop at a single course? Embrace a culture of continuous education, where learning is as much a part of your routine as your morning coffee. ChatGPT allows you to explore diverse educational opportunities that keep your mind engaged and your skills sharp. Consider pursuing certifications or degrees that align with your passions or career aspirations. After all, it's never too late to add a new feather to your cap. Personal development courses are another avenue to explore, offering insights into everything from time management to emotional intelligence. Picture yourself in a virtual classroom, engaging with like-minded individuals worldwide, each lesson a step toward personal growth. It's an ongoing process that enriches your life and broadens your horizons, all from the comfort of your home.

Learning is most effective when supported by study aids and a well-structured schedule. ChatGPT can help you create these tools, ensuring your educational journey is organized and enjoyable. Imagine using flashcard creation tools to memorize new vocabulary or concepts, each card a stepping stone toward mastery. Or perhaps you prefer the camaraderie of a study group, where ideas flow as freely as a good conversation. ChatGPT can assist in coordinating these groups and connecting you with peers who share your interests and goals. Together, you can tackle challenging topics, share insights, and support one another's progress. It's a community effort that makes learning a solitary pursuit and a shared adventure.

Sharing your learning experiences with others adds a rich layer to the educational process. Picture engaging in online discussion forums to exchange ideas and perspectives with fellow learners. It's like sitting around a virtual campfire, each person contributing their unique story to the collective narrative. Virtual presentation sessions offer another platform for sharing knowledge, allowing you to showcase what you've learned and receive feedback from a diverse audience. These interactions deepen your understanding and build confidence in your ability to communicate and teach others. It's a rewarding cycle of giving and receiving that enhances the learning experience for everyone involved.

Evaluating courses and instructors is crucial in maximizing your online learning experience. ChatGPT can guide you in assessing course quality and instructor credentials, helping you make informed decisions. Picture perusing course review sites, much like reading book reviews before diving into a new novel. These insights provide a glimpse into what you can expect, helping you choose courses that align with your expectations and learning style. Instructor background checks add another layer of assurance, ensuring you're learning from knowledgeable and credible educators. With ChatGPT's assistance, you can navigate these options confidently, selecting courses that offer both challenge and fulfillment.

As you immerse yourself in online classes, remember that learning is a lifelong journey that evolves with every new experience and discovery. Embrace the opportunities before you, knowing that each class and lesson is a step toward a more prosperous, more fulfilled life. Whether mastering a new skill or exploring an old interest, the world of knowledge is at your fingertips, waiting to be explored.

Reader Reviver Brain Break

Let this moment be delightfully unserious. The gnome isn't judging. He's just here to hold the question-and maybe giggle into his beard.

We spend so much time being productive, correct, and efficient. But play is powerful, too.

So what if your following prompt makes no sense at all? What if it's just... fun?

Ask something ridiculous. Like "Do penguins have best friends?" or "Could AI write a love letter to my toaster?"

Then sip your tea and wait for the answer. Curiosity is a superpower – even when it's silly.

Safety and Privacy in the Digital Age

Let's take a little stroll down memory lane, shall we? Remember when privacy meant drawing the curtains and ensuring the neighbors weren't peeking in? Today, privacy has become a digital affair, like trying to keep secrets in a fishbowl. Understanding data privacy in the age of AI is crucial, especially regarding tools like ChatGPT. Imagine ChatGPT as your chatty friend who somehow knows a bit about everything under the sun. But how does it get all that information? AI systems like ChatGPT collect data to improve their services. This data collection process is like your favorite aunt, who only takes what she needs for her famous apple pie recipe, leaving out anything unnecessary. The focus is on usage rather than personal data, meaning it's more about understanding patterns and less about knowing your deepest secrets.

Now, let's talk about data anonymization, which is a fancy way of saying that personal identifiers are stripped away from the data collected. Think of it like sending a letter without a return address. This process ensures that while the AI learns and adapts, it doesn't know who you are. It's like conversing at a crowded party where you can discuss various topics without revealing personal details. It's comforting to know that while AI is learning and evolving, your privacy remains intact, much like that secret recipe you share only with close friends.

Ah, privacy policies are the fine print we all love to skip. But here's the thing: understanding these policies is vital. They're like the rulebook to a board game, ensuring everyone plays fair. A good privacy policy outlines what data is collected, how it's used, and with whom it's shared. It's like knowing where your luggage goes when you check it at the airport.

On the other hand, terms of service highlight your rights and responsibilities as a user. They're the equivalent of understanding that you can't just waltz into a restaurant and help yourself to the chef's special. By reading these documents, you empower yourself with knowledge, ensuring no surprises.

Let's delve into the world of data encryption, another layer of protection for your digital interactions. Encryption is like having a conversation in code, only understandable to those with the key. End-to-end encryption ensures that your messages are secured from when they leave your device until they reach their destination. It's like passing notes in class that only your best friend can read. SSL/TLS protocols add another layer of security, acting like a secure tunnel through which your data travels safely. It's akin to sending your prized possessions through a trusted courier who guarantees delivery without peeking inside.

With all the talk about data privacy, it's natural to have some lingering concerns. You've probably heard about data misuse and privacy breaches, which can send shivers down anyone's spine. However, the AI industry is making strides to address these issues. Compliance with global regulations, such as GDPR in Europe, ensures that companies adhere to strict data protection standards. It's like having a watchdog that ensures everyone's playing by the rules. Industry certifications further reinforce trust, acting like a seal of approval that companies are committed to safeguarding your privacy.

In this digital age, privacy isn't just a luxury – it's a necessity. As you navigate the online world, remember that understanding how your data is used and protected empowers you. And who knows? It might even make reading privacy policies a tad more interesting, like discovering the plot twist in your favorite mystery novel. So, armed with this knowledge, go forth and explore the wonders of AI, knowing that your privacy is a priority, just like those secret family recipes passed down through generations.

Protecting Your Personal Information: Best Practices

Ever found yourself standing in the kitchen, trying to remember if you turned off the stove before stepping out? That nagging worry is similar to how we should feel about digital security. Developing strong password habits is essential - think of them as the locks on your digital doors. Gone are the days when "password123" would suffice. Today, a good password should be long, complex, and unique. But let's face it, remembering all those intricate combinations can feel like trying to memorize the names of all your second cousins. This is where password managers come to the rescue. They're like a well-organized spice rack for your digital life, storing all your passwords securely and helping you generate new ones as strong as an ox. According to recommendations from cybersecurity experts like Gunnar Kallstrom, tools like 1Password or Dashlane can simplify your life, ensuring you remember only one master password (Source 2).

Let's sprinkle in some extra security with two-factor authentication (2FA). Imagine it as a double-lock system for your online accounts. You enter your password and then get a text message with a code. It's like your digital version of having a bouncer outside a VIP room, ensuring only you get access. This extra step can protect you from unauthorized access, giving you peace of mind when browsing the web. Implementing this is usually straightforward – just look for the 2FA option in your account settings and follow the prompts. It's a small step that can make a huge difference in keeping your information safe.

Now, let's talk about phishing attempts. These are like the digital equivalent of a scam artist trying to sell you a bridge. They often come in emails that look legitimate but aim to steal your personal information. Spotting these pesky scams can save you a lot of heartache. Look out for common indicators, like urgent requests for information, suspicious links, or email addresses that don't match the company they claim to be from. Practice safe email habits by never clicking links or downloading attachments from unknown sources. If an email looks fishy, trust your gut and verify its authenticity by contacting the company directly. Staying vigilant helps keep your information out of the wrong hands.

When you're out and about, sipping coffee at your favorite café and connecting to the free public Wi-Fi is tempting. But beware! Public networks can be as insecure as a leaky rowboat. Hackers can easily intercept data on these networks, so using secure connections is crucial when accessing sensitive information. Enter VPNs or Virtual Private Networks, like cloaks of invisibility for your internet activity. They encrypt your data and hide your online presence, making it much harder for prying eyes to see what you're up to. Consider using a reputable VPN service whenever you're on public Wi-Fi, ensuring your online activities remain as private as a secret sandwich recipe.

Finally, staying updated on security practices is akin to keeping your car in tune with regular oil changes and tire checks. The digital landscape is constantly evolving, and so are the threats. Keeping informed about the latest cybersecurity news can help you stay one step ahead of potential risks. There are numerous online resources and courses available to enhance your cybersecurity knowledge. Whether a quick article or an in-depth online course, these resources empower you to protect yourself and your family in our increasingly digital world. By embracing these best practices, you can confidently navigate the digital realm, knowing your personal information is secure.

Configuring Security Settings in ChatGPT

Imagine stepping into a new car for the first time. Before taking off, you'd adjust the mirrors and set the radio to your favorite station, right? Configuring security settings in

ChatGPT is a bit like that. First, you'll want to access the security settings. Start by navigating to the settings menu - usually represented by a gear icon. Once there, you'll find options that let you tailor your experience. It's like choosing the perfect playlist for a road trip. Adjust privacy controls to decide what you're comfortable sharing. Not every setting will be relevant to everyone, so feel free to tweak them to fit your unique needs, much like adjusting the seat to your height.

Customizing user preferences is where you get your stamp on the experience. It's akin to adding those little knick-knacks in your living space that make it feel like home. In the settings, you can find notification options. Maybe you prefer a gentle ping for updates rather than a loud chime. Adjust these settings to ensure ChatGPT communicates in a way that suits you. Data-sharing options allow you to choose how much or how little you want to disclose. It's like deciding whether to keep your curtains open or closed – personal comfort is key.

Implementing parental controls is wise for those with young explorers at home. It's like setting boundaries for playtime, ensuring your little ones stay safe online. Look for content filtering tools in the settings. These tools act as gatekeepers, blocking inappropriate content and keeping the digital environment friendly. Usage monitoring features are another handy addition, allowing you to keep tabs on how much time is spent engaging with ChatGPT. Your digital nanny will watch over your kids while they navigate the vast world of AI.

Now, talk about backing up data – an often overlooked but crucial step. Think of it as creating a safety net. Regularly backing up your data ensures you won't lose everything if things go awry. Cloud storage solutions are popular, allowing access to your data from anywhere. Imagine it as a virtual attic where all your important documents are safely stored.

External hard drives are another option, providing a physical backup that you can keep close at hand. It's like having a spare key to your house, reassuring you that you have a backup plan in emergencies.

Checklist for Configuring ChatGPT Security Settings

These steps ensure you have complete control over your ChatGPT experience, just as you would with any other aspect of your daily life. By taking the time to configure these settings, you create a personalized, secure, and enjoyable environment for yourself and your family.

Recognizing and Avoiding Online Scams

In our bustling digital age, the internet can sometimes feel like the Wild West - a frontier filled with opportunity but not without its outlaws. Online scams are as varied as they are sneaky, with scammers donning the disguise of legitimate AI service providers or tech support angels. Imagine receiving an email from someone claiming to be from a well-known tech company, offering to fix a "critical problem" on your computer. It sounds plausible at first, but these fraudulent tech support scams are nothing more than wolves in sheep's clothing. They may ask you to install software or provide remote access, which can be as dangerous as handing your house keys to a stranger. Meanwhile, fake AI service providers might promise miraculous results, offering services that sound too good to be true – and they often are. Before you know it, you could be caught in a web spun by a scammer eager to exploit your trust and curiosity.

So, how do you dodge these digital pickpockets? It starts with knowing the signs and keeping your wits about you. Genuine companies won't ask for personal information via email or phone, especially without verifying your identity. If you receive a suspicious request, pause and investigate before acting. Use official channels to contact the company directly and confirm if the request is genuine. It's like verifying a juicy rumor by asking the source instead of relying on the grapevine. This cautious approach, aptly dubbed "trust but verify," can save you from unnecessary headaches and potential data breaches.

Reporting it can help protect others from falling into the same trap if you stumble upon a scam. Think of it as calling in the cavalry to round up the outlaws. You can report suspicious activity to relevant authorities, such as the Federal Trade Commission (FTC) or your country's equivalent. Many platforms also offer reporting tools, allowing you to flag fraudulent emails or websites with just a few clicks. By taking these steps, you're protecting yourself and contributing to a safer online community for everyone. It's like being a digital vigilante, helping keep the internet free from ne'er-do-wells.

Education is your best ally in the fight against scams. Staying informed about new tactics keeps you a step ahead of the tricksters. Consider attending scam awareness workshops or community education initiatives, which are as enlightening as a good whodunit novel. These sessions often share the latest scam trends, teaching you how to spot the red flags before you find yourself in a sticky situation. Community discussions also provide a platform to share experiences and tips, reinforcing the notion that knowledge is power.

Empowerment through vigilance is the mantra to live by. While it's tempting to assume the best of people, a healthy dose of skepticism is wise when navigating the digital landscape. Always ensure you interact with official websites and sources, like choosing a reputable café for your morning coffee over a dubious roadside stall. This discernment protects your personal information and ensures that you can enjoy the benefits of technology without the lurking fear of scams. It's about balancing curiosity and caution, allowing you to explore the digital world with confidence and peace of mind.

Safeguarding Conversations: Ensuring Privacy

Imagine chatting with your neighbor over the garden fence, but you'd prefer if the entire street didn't overhear. Securing your conversations digitally is like that - a way to keep the chat cozy and private. In the vast world of AI, secure messaging protocols are your first line of defense. They act like soundproof walls, ensuring your conversation remains between you and the intended recipient. Encryption plays a vital role here, wrapping your messages in a digital cloak so that even if someone did eavesdrop, all they'd hear is gibberish. Think of it like sending a letter in code; only the recipient has the decryption key.

But what happens when the conversation is over? Managing your conversation history is as important as securing the chat itself. It's akin to tidying up after a lively dinner party. Deletion settings come in handy here. They allow you to remove chats no longer needed, like clearing out old receipts from your wallet. In ChatGPT, you can adjust these settings to automatically delete conversations after a certain period, ensuring your chat history doesn't become a digital clutter. Archiving those conversations you wish to keep is a smart move. This way, essential discussions are filed away for future reference, like storing unique letters in a shoebox under your bed.

When sharing information through AI platforms, less is definitely more. Imagine an AI chat as a friendly conversation with a stranger on a train. You wouldn't spill your life story or financial details to someone you just met, would you? Keep personal identification details, like your Social Security number or home address, under wraps. Similarly, avoid sharing financial information, like credit card numbers or bank account details. By limiting what you share, you maintain control over your personal narrative, ensuring that sensitive information remains as private as a secret recipe.

Finally, let's chat about consent and privacy – an essential part of any information-sharing scenario. When you're about to share information about others, obtaining their consent is crucial. Imagine it like borrowing a friend's car; you wouldn't take it for a spin without asking. The legal aspects of data sharing emphasize this point, reminding us that sharing someone else's information without permission can lead to complications. Ethical considerations also come into play, encouraging us to treat others' information with the same care and respect we expect. This approach fosters trust and promotes a culture of privacy and respect in our digital interactions.

Trusting AI: Building Confidence in Technology

Imagine you're at a bustling farmers' market, where transparency is key. You want to know exactly where your produce comes from, and the farmers are happy to share every detail. In the world of AI, transparency is just as crucial. Companies work tirelessly to ensure you, the user, can trust their technologies. Public transparency reports have become a staple, offering insights into how AI systems operate and what data they handle. Think of it as having a clear window into their processes, ensuring nothing is hidden. Open-source AI initiatives further bolster this trust, allowing experts worldwide to scrutinize and improve AI systems. It's the digital equivalent of an open kitchen, where the chefs are happy to share their recipes and techniques for all to see.

AI's positive applications are vast and varied, touching nearly every facet of our lives. In healthcare, AI-driven tools have revolutionized diagnostics, making early detection of diseases more accurate and speedy. Imagine an AI system that scans medical images with the precision of a seasoned doctor, helping pinpoint issues that might be missed by the human eye. This isn't just science fiction; it's happening today, saving lives and improving outcomes. Education, too, has seen a boon from AI's capabilities. Personalized learning platforms adapt to each student's pace, making complex subjects accessible to all. Imagine it as having a tutor who knows exactly where you struggle and how to guide you, ensuring no one gets left behind.

However, it's vital to acknowledge AI's limitations and the responsibilities that come with its use. AI isn't infallible. It can be biased, reflecting the data it's trained on. Understanding AI bias is essential for users and developers alike. It’s like recognizing the potential for a favorite recipe to go awry if one ingredient is off. Users of AI, including chatbots like ChatGPT, are responsible for engaging ethically. This means being mindful of shared information and understanding that AI is a tool, not a sentient being. It's crucial to remember that while AI can offer suggestions, the final decision should always rest with you. This responsibility resembles steering a ship; the AI can chart potential courses, but you hold the wheel.

Approaching AI with an open mind unlocks its myriad benefits. Many success stories highlight AI's potential to transform lives and industries. The possibilities are endless, from agricultural innovations that optimize crop yields to AI-driven financial tools that help manage investments. These case studies show that AI isn't just a futuristic concept but a present-day ally. As technology evolves, so too does AI's potential. Future developments promise even more groundbreaking applications, making it an exciting field to watch. Imagine a world where AI assists in daily chores, offers companionship, or helps solve global challenges. The future is bright, and AI is a significant part of that promise.

The key is to foster a positive perspective on AI, seeing it as a partner in progress rather than a threat. By understanding its capabilities and limitations, you can leverage AI to enhance your life. Approach each interaction with curiosity, openness, and skepticism, ensuring you get the best from technology. As we conclude this chapter, remember that AI is here to stay, and by embracing it, you become part of a forward-thinking community ready to tackle tomorrow's challenges. In the next chapter, we'll explore how technology intersects with lifelong learning, ensuring that, no matter your age, there's always something new to discover.

Reader Reviver Brain Break

Let this question linger like honey on a spoon. Sweet. Slow. Familiar.

The old hive lid holding this card once covered something golden - and so does your memory.

Think of a café booth, a back veranda, or a kitchen table. What sound was in the background? Who was across from you? What was in your cup?

Let the memory rise. You don't need to write it all down – just feel it. Because the best parts of technology are the ones that help us remember that we are human.

Interactive and Engaging Content

It's a lazy Sunday afternoon, and you're sipping on a cup of your favorite brew, pondering how far you've come with this whole ChatGPT adventure. Maybe you've already regaled your grandkids with tales of the IBM Memory Typewriter or blown their minds with your newfound knack for tech lingo. But there's always more to learn, isn't there? Just like when you thought you'd mastered ballroom dancing, only to realize there was a new step to conquer! This chapter is your dance floor, and we're about to introduce a fun twist – interactive quizzes designed to test your ChatGPT knowledge and keep those mental cogs turning.

Quizzes might take you back to school days, but these aren't your average pop quizzes. Instead, consider them a friendly challenge to solidify your understanding while having fun. We'll start by engaging multiple-choice questions that cover the basics of ChatGPT's features and applications. Imagine yourself as a game show contestant, confidently buzzing in as you identify the correct commands for various tasks. What does ChatGPT do when you ask it to draft an email? How does it respond to a request for historical trivia? Each question is crafted to reinforce those key concepts you've been learning along the way.

But variety is the spice of life, and our quizzes aren't just about picking the right option. You'll encounter true or false questions that delve into the nitty-gritty of privacy settings – because we all know how important it is to keep our digital lives secure. And then, there are fill-in-the-blank questions that challenge you to recall specific features or commands, ensuring that your knowledge is broad and deep. Mixing up the question formats, we cater to different learning preferences, ensuring everyone finds a way to engage and enjoy.

Now, let's talk feedback. Instant feedback is crucial, especially when eager to learn and improve. Each quiz offers immediate explanations for the answers, helping you understand the correct choice and why it was the right one. It's like having a personal tutor gently guiding you towards greater understanding. And suppose you feel like you need a little extra help. In that case, links to additional resources are just a click away, offering further reading and exploration.

Of course, practice makes perfect, and these quizzes are designed to encourage repeat attempts. Maybe you didn't ace it the first time – no worries! Each time you retake a quiz, you'll reinforce your learning and track your progress with helpful tools that show how far you've come. And to keep things exciting, score improvement incentives are in place, turning learning into a rewarding experience. Picture a little cheer from ChatGPT every time you beat your previous score – it's like having a virtual fan club rooting for your success.

Progress Tracker

Consider keeping a progress tracker to visualize your learning journey. When you complete a quiz, mark your score and jot down a quick note on what you learned or want to revisit. Over time, you'll see a clear picture of your growth, which is motivating and satisfying.

PROGRESS TRACKER

Quiz	Score	Notes
Quiz 1		
Quiz 2		
Quiz 3		
Quiz 4		

So, dive into these interactive quizzes with curiosity and a sense of adventure. They're more than just tests – they're stepping stones on your path to becoming a ChatGPT virtuoso. Whether you're asking questions or learning from mistakes, each quiz is an opportunity to deepen your understanding and build confidence in your abilities. Remember, every great dancer starts with a few missteps, so embrace the process and enjoy the journey.

Who knows? You might just surprise yourself with how much you've learned and how eager you are to keep exploring.

Practical Exercises: Applying ChatGPT in Real-Life

Imagine sitting at your desk, staring at a blank page, knowing it's time to plan the next virtual family reunion. The thought might seem daunting, but with ChatGPT by your side, it's like having a seasoned event planner whispering brilliant ideas in your ear. Start by using ChatGPT to draft a meeting agenda. You can ask it to help you organize topics, suggest discussion points, and even include a few icebreakers to get everyone chatting. Picture this: your family logs into the virtual meet, and instead of the usual chaos, there's a structured plan in place, making the gathering as smooth as your morning coffee.

Now, let's switch gears to another scenario. Perhaps you've been roped into drafting the monthly community newsletter. This task might feel a bit like juggling flaming torches. Fear not. With ChatGPT, you have the ultimate assistant. Begin with a simple prompt: "Draft a community newsletter for April." Watch as ChatGPT generates a template with sections for events, community news, and a spotlight on local heroes. It's like having a skilled editor at your fingertips, guiding you through the process quickly. Add a personal flair, and you'll have a newsletter the neighborhood will be eager to read.

Let's clarify it for those who like to see things step-by-step. Suppose you're planning that virtual family meeting. Start by opening ChatGPT and entering your initial prompt. As it generates ideas, jot them down in a document. Next, arrange the topics in a logical order, adding any personal notes or reminders. If you're drafting that newsletter, begin with an outline. Let ChatGPT suggest headlines or catchy phrases, then flesh out each section with details. Use visual aids like bullet points or charts to keep information clear and engaging.

But don’t stop there. Encourage yourself to think outside the box. Maybe there's a problem you’ve been pondering, like how to make family game nights more exciting or how to organize a charity fundraiser. Use ChatGPT to brainstorm creative solutions or innovative approaches. It can suggest unique themes, activities, or fundraising ideas to spark interest and excitement. Picture yourself as an innovator, using ChatGPT to turn everyday challenges into opportunities for creativity and fun.

Sharing is caring, as they say, and fostering a collaborative learning environment can be incredibly rewarding. After completing these exercises, consider discussing your outcomes with friends or family. Perhaps you’ve created a stellar newsletter – why not share it in an online discussion forum or a community Facebook group? Gather feedback, exchange ideas, and inspire someone else to try it. Peer feedback sessions can enlighten, reveal new perspectives, or offer constructive tips. Imagine the satisfaction of knowing your work has met your goals and inspired others.

Why not create a virtual meeting agenda or community newsletter using ChatGPT? Share your completed work with a friend or community group and ask for feedback.

Notice how collaboration and sharing enhance the experience, making it more enriching and enjoyable.

Incorporating ChatGPT into real-life scenarios isn't just about ticking off tasks; it's about transforming ordinary moments into extraordinary experiences. Whether planning events, drafting documents, or dreaming up new ideas, ChatGPT adds a touch of magic, making each task a little brighter and much more manageable. So, explore these practical exercises with an open heart and a curious mind. Who knows what you'll accomplish with some help from your AI friend?

Real-World Challenges: Solving Common Problems

Imagine your daily schedule as a jazz band, each task playing its instrument, hoping to create harmony rather than noise. But sometimes, it feels more like a cacophony of clashing cymbals and wayward trumpets. Keeping everything in sync can be challenging, especially when life throws in surprise solos, like an unexpected visit from the grandkids or a last-minute invite to a community event. This is where ChatGPT steps in, offering its digital baton to help orchestrate your day. Managing a busy schedule doesn't have to feel like herding cats. With the correct prompts, ChatGPT can assist in prioritizing tasks, setting reminders, and even suggesting efficient ways to allocate your time. Think of it as having a personal assistant who never forgets a birthday and always knows when to water the plants. ChatGPT turns your daily chaos into a well-rehearsed symphony by automating tasks like sending reminders for bills or scheduling doctor appointments.

Organizing digital photos can often feel like wading through a sea of snapshots, each a captured moment, yet somehow lost in the digital ether. Remember the days of flipping through photo albums, each page a curated journey through time? Now, with smartphones and digital cameras, our collections have grown exponentially, yet finding that perfect picture from last summer's beach trip can feel like searching for a needle in a haystack. ChatGPT can help bring order to this digital chaos. By suggesting categorization techniques, such as tagging photos with dates, locations, or themes like "Family Reunions" or "Adventure Days," ChatGPT helps transform your digital hodgepodge into a neatly organized gallery. Imagine effortlessly pulling up photos from every family vacation or those candid snaps of the grandkids, ready to share at a moment's notice.

Engaging in problem-solving sessions can be the perfect way to tackle these challenges head-on, turning them into opportunities for growth and learning. Picture a live Q&A session, where you and fellow learners gather to share tips and tricks, each question leading to a new discovery. It's like a virtual coffee klatch, where everyone brings their puzzle pieces, and you create a complete picture together. Interactive webinars can also be a fantastic resource, offering hands-on guidance and practical advice.

With experts leading the way, these sessions become a treasure trove of knowledge, equipping you with the tools you need to tackle your digital dilemmas confidently.

Reflection is a powerful tool in reinforcing learning and growth. Consider taking a moment each day to reflect on the challenges you've faced and the solutions you've discovered. Reflective journaling prompts can guide you, encouraging you to jot down your thoughts and insights. You might start with, "What was one challenge I overcame today, and how did I feel afterward?" This simple reflection reinforces your learning and provides a sense of accomplishment. Discussing lessons learned with others can further enhance this experience, offering fresh perspectives and fostering community. Imagine sitting with a group of friends, each sharing their reflections, much like a book club but with a focus on personal growth and practical learning.

Incorporating these practices into your life helps solve the challenges at hand. It empowers you with the skills to tackle future obstacles. With ChatGPT as your guide, you're not just learning to manage your schedule or organize your photos; you're building a toolkit of strategies and insights that can be applied to countless areas of life. Each problem becomes a stepping stone, leading you to greater confidence and capability. Whether transforming your daily routine into a masterpiece of efficiency or crafting a digital album that captures the essence of family life, you can handle it all with a smile and a sense of adventure.

Creating Your Own ChatGPT Scenarios

Picture yourself at a family gathering, where grandkids dash about, and adults converse. Imagine turning this lively scene into a scenario where ChatGPT plays a part in enhancing the experience. The beauty of creating your own ChatGPT scenarios is that it opens up a world of possibilities, allowing you to explore its potential in ways uniquely suited to your needs. Begin by thinking about scenario planning as a fun project. Use templates to outline what you want to achieve. It could be a way to plan a family game night or perhaps a tool to help organize your following travel itinerary. Crafting your own scenarios is a bit like drawing a roadmap, with each step leading to a destination of your choice. Consider what you want to accomplish, and let ChatGPT be your guide on this adventure.

But don't stop there. Once you have a rough outline, it's time to unleash your creativity. This is where the real magic happens. Allow yourself to think outside the box and develop scenarios that meet your goals and inspire new ways of thinking. Perhaps you'll brainstorm a scenario where ChatGPT assists in planning a surprise party, complete with a playlist of your favorite tunes and a menu of nostalgic treats. Or maybe you'll dream up an imaginative role-playing game where ChatGPT becomes a character in your story, guiding you through challenges and offering hints. The key is to let your imagination run wild and see where it takes you. Think of it as a blank canvas, with ChatGPT providing the colors and brushes.

Now, let's test those scenarios. It's one thing to imagine how ChatGPT might work in a given situation, but putting it to the test is where you truly see its capabilities. Create checklists to ensure each element of your scenario is covered from start to finish. Consider your feedback during testing as valuable insights that help refine and improve your scenario. It's like baking a cake - sometimes, you must tweak the recipe to get it right. Gather feedback from those who participate, whether family members, friends, or online communities. Their perspectives can offer new ideas or highlight areas that need adjustment. Embrace the feedback process to enhance your scenarios and make them even more effective.

Sharing your creations with others is rewarding and an excellent way to collaborate and learn. Join scenario exchange networks or workshops where you can present your ideas and receive constructive input. This collaboration allows you to refine your scenarios, incorporating fresh perspectives you might not have considered. It's like a potluck dinner where everyone brings a dish, creating a feast of ideas that benefit everyone involved. You might find yourself inspired by someone else's scenario, leading you to modify your own in a way that makes it even better. The spirit of collaboration fosters creativity and growth, making creating and sharing scenarios a fulfilling experience.

Creating your own ChatGPT scenarios is about exploring possibilities and discovering new ways to incorporate technology into your life. It's about taking the reins and tailoring ChatGPT's capabilities to fit your unique needs and interests. Whether planning an event, solving a problem, or simply exploring new ideas, your scenarios can be as dynamic and diverse as your imagination allows. So, embrace the challenge, unleash your creativity, and see where your scenarios take you.

Building Confidence Through Hands-On Practice

Imagine you're in your favorite chair, the one that hugs you just right, and you're about to try something new with ChatGPT. Perhaps you're feeling excitement and apprehension, like the first time you rode a bike without training wheels. The key to building confidence with technology is active learning – rolling up your sleeves and diving right in. Think of self-guided practice sessions as your personal playground, where you can experiment with ChatGPT's features at your own pace. These sessions are like gentle strolls through a park, allowing you to explore without the pressure of onlookers. Interactive tutorials can also offer structured guidance, providing a roadmap to navigate more complex tasks. They're akin to having a friendly guide by your side, pointing out interesting landmarks and ensuring you don't get lost.

Real-time feedback is a game-changer when learning something new. It's like having a wise mentor who taps you on the shoulder and says, "Try this instead," just before you make a wrong turn. Instantaneous feedback mechanisms help you adjust your approach on the spot, offering suggestions to improve your skills. Imagine you're crafting a message with ChatGPT, and it gently nudges you to refine your tone or tweak a phrase for clarity. These minor adjustments build your competence and ensure each interaction is a learning opportunity. Over time, you'll make fewer mistakes and gain more confidence, much like a baker who finally nails that stubborn soufflé recipe.

Creating a supportive environment is crucial. Picture a cozy book club where everyone shares their thoughts without judgment, and every idea is met with encouragement. This is the atmosphere we aim to foster as you explore ChatGPT. Peer support groups can provide a sense of community, where you can share your experiences and learn from others. Whether it's an online forum or a local tech meetup, being part of a group that shares your interests and challenges makes the learning process feel less daunting. Community mentors can also offer advice and encouragement as cheerleaders who celebrate your progress and motivate you to keep going. Their guidance and support can transform a solitary endeavor into a shared journey, making each step feel lighter and more enjoyable.

Celebrating small wins is a cornerstone of building confidence. It's like savoring a piece of chocolate after a long walk – a moment to pause and acknowledge your efforts. Every achievement, no matter how small, is a milestone worth celebrating. Maybe you've successfully used ChatGPT to draft an email or plan a family event. Take a moment to recognize your progress. Share your success stories with others, whether it's a post in an online community or a conversation with a friend over coffee. These stories boost your confidence and inspire others to embark on learning adventures. Acknowledging your achievements reinforces a positive mindset that encourages further exploration and growth.

Incorporating these practices into your learning routine transforms the process into a rewarding experience. Hands-on practice empowers you with the skills and confidence to tackle new challenges. At the same time, real-time feedback and support create a nurturing environment for growth. Celebrating your successes, however small, reinforces your achievements and motivates you to continue exploring. With ChatGPT as your companion, you're not just learning to use a tool – you're building the confidence to embrace new possibilities and enrich your life. So, as you sit in your favorite chair, ready to take on the next challenge, remember that each step forward is a step towards mastering something new.

Evaluating Your Progress and Growth

There's nothing like seeing how far you've come when learning something new. It's like looking back at old family photos and seeing how the kids have grown. Self-assessment tools can be your mirror, reflecting your progress with ChatGPT in an encouraging and enlightening way. You might start with a self-evaluation questionnaire, a simple way to capture where and where you're headed. It's a chance to ask yourself questions like, "What features have I mastered?" or "Which areas still puzzle me?" By taking stock of your skills in a structured way, you can celebrate your victories and pinpoint areas for improvement.

Progress dashboards are another fantastic tool, offering a visual snapshot of your journey. Imagine a colorful chart tracking your growth, with each bar representing a new skill or milestone achieved. It would be a scrapbook of your ChatGPT adventures that paints a picture of progress and potential. These dashboards allow you to see trends over time, helping you understand what you've learned and how you've evolved. With each new achievement, you add another brushstroke to your tapestry of learning, crafting a masterpiece that showcases your dedication and growth.

Setting goals is much like charting a course for a road trip. You need a destination (a skill you want to master) and a roadmap (a plan). Goal-setting frameworks can help you map out this journey, offering a structured way to define your objectives. Whether you're aiming to become a whiz at ChatGPT's advanced features or to streamline your daily tasks, setting clear, realistic goals is the key. And just like any good road trip, reviewing and adjusting your route is essential. Reflect on your progress regularly, making necessary changes to ensure you're on the right path.

Feedback is a gift, and creating opportunities to receive constructive input can be invaluable. Consider joining virtual learning communities where fellow learners share insights and offer advice. It's like sitting around a campfire, swapping stories and learning from each other's experiences. You might also seek professional evaluation services, where experts provide detailed feedback on your skills. These evaluations can offer a fresh perspective, highlighting strengths and growth areas. By embracing feedback as a tool for improvement, you turn each comment into a stepping stone toward mastery.

Reflecting on your learning journey is more than just a retrospective glance; it's an opportunity to connect the dots of your experiences. Reflective learning diaries can be your faithful companion, capturing thoughts and insights. Imagine a journal filled with your personal growth stories, each entry a testament to your resilience and curiosity. As you flip through its pages, you'll see the narrative of your learning unfold, revealing the challenges you've overcome and the triumphs you've celebrated. This reflection solidifies your understanding and inspires you to continue exploring new horizons.

As we draw this chapter close, let's take a moment to recognize the power of progress and growth. You've engaged with interactive content, crafted scenarios, and built confidence through hands-on practice. Each step has added depth to your understanding, transforming you into a more confident and capable ChatGPT user. With these tools, you're ready to tackle new challenges and explore even greater possibilities. Let's continue this adventure as we move into the next chapter, where we'll delve into the exciting world of maximizing productivity and monetizing your ideas with ChatGPT.

Reader Reviver Brain Break

Imagine a tiny ballerina twirling to a melody tucked away in your memory. Let the invisible music slow your thoughts. This is not the moment for productivity – it's a moment for stillness.

Close your eyes and hum a tune from childhood, or let ChatGPT help you find a lullaby from the decade you were born. Don't rush. Let the notes settle the noise.

Let the question spark a smile, a memory, or a giggle.

You can ponder silently, jot a quick note in the margin, or share your answer with a friend over coffee.

Like winding a music box, take a moment to breathe, stretch, and soften. Let the mental music guide you back to the page with fresh energy.

No rush. Just rhythm.

Optional ChatGPT Prompt: "Can you find a nostalgic lullaby or soft piano piece from the (enter your birth decade here) I might enjoy unwinding to?"

Empowerment and Exploration

Picture yourself standing at the edge of a vast, shimmering digital ocean. It's as if the world has transformed into a grand treasure map, each corner hiding tools, insights, and the promise of new friendships. But, like any great adventure, this exploration begins with a whisper of trepidation – a little voice echoing, "Can I truly navigate these digital waters?" You're not alone. This chapter is for you, dear reader, as we take a gentle, supportive stroll through overcoming tech anxiety, embracing the wonders that await with ChatGPT, and transforming apprehension into curiosity.

Embracing the Adventure: Overcoming Tech Anxiety

Let's talk about tech anxiety - the sneaky gremlin that seems to pop up whenever you face a new gadget or app. It's not uncommon to feel a bit of dread when technology changes faster than a teenager's hairstyle. You might notice a flutter of panic at the thought of pressing the wrong button or a sense of overwhelm as information bombards you from every angle. These are telltale signs of tech anxiety, a natural response to the rapid pace of digital evolution. Understanding these feelings is the first step in taming them, allowing you to reclaim the joy of discovery.

The key to overcoming this anxiety lies in gentle, gradual exposure. Imagine dipping your toes into a chilly pool, letting the water warm around you before diving in. Begin with small, manageable tasks. Perhaps try sending a simple message with ChatGPT or asking it to find a recipe for your next Sunday roast. These small victories build confidence, showing you that technology isn't an obstacle but a helpful companion. Couple this with mindfulness exercises. Picture yourself pausing to take a deep breath, centering your thoughts, and reminding yourself that exploring at your own pace is okay. A calm mind is your best ally in tackling tech.

Cultivating a growth mindset can also transform your tech journey. Instead of viewing mistakes as failures, see them as stepping stones to mastery. Remember your first attempt at riding a bicycle? Wobbles and falls were part of the process; each taught you something new. Apply this mindset to technology. Set small, incremental goals - like mastering a new feature on ChatGPT each week. Celebrate these achievements, no matter how minor they may seem. Each step forward is a testament to your resilience and adaptability, which have carried you through many adventures.

I want to share a story about Helen, a spirited 68-year-old passionate about gardening. Helen hesitated when her grandchildren introduced her to ChatGPT, fearing she'd never grasp it. But with gentle encouragement, she began asking ChatGPT about plant care tips. Each interaction boosted her confidence. Now, she uses ChatGPT to plan her garden and engages in lively conversations with her grandkids about tech. Helen's journey from apprehension to enthusiasm is a testament to the power of perseverance and the joy of learning.

Reflection Section

Take a moment to jot down one tech-related goal you'd like to achieve this month. Use ChatGPT to help outline the steps needed. Each week, reflect on your progress and note any insights gained. Celebrate each milestone, no matter how small.

These stories and strategies illustrate that tech anxiety is merely a temporary guest that can be shown the door with patience, practice, and a sprinkle of humor. Embrace this adventure, knowing that you're not just learning technology with each step but expanding your world.

Empowering Yourself Through Technology

Imagine a world where you navigate technology with the ease of a seasoned sailor, charting new courses in your personal and professional life. Embracing technology offers a gateway to increased independence, allowing you to manage daily tasks with newfound efficiency. Picture yourself video chatting with family halfway across the globe, sharing stories and laughter as if they were beside you. Or envision using online platforms to tackle everything from banking to booking vacations, all with a few clicks. Technology isn't just a tool; it's a bridge to greater freedom and self-sufficiency, enhancing your communication skills in ways you never thought possible.

Now, explore the treasure trove of resources available to aid your self-empowerment journey. Online learning platforms, like **Udemy** or **Coursera**, offer courses in virtually any field you can imagine – from cooking to coding. These platforms are a boon, especially for those who relish learning at their own pace with a cup of coffee. Then, productivity apps like **Evernote** or **Todoist** help you organize your tasks and thoughts. Imagine these apps as your personal assistants, always ready to remind you of a meeting or make a grocery list. They transform your smartphone or tablet into a powerhouse of productivity, allowing you to reclaim time and focus on what truly matters.

However, empowerment also means advocating for your tech needs within your circle. It's crucial to clearly communicate what you require to feel confident and capable at home or in the workplace. Discuss your tech needs with family members, who might be more than willing to offer guidance or suggest user-friendly gadgets tailored to your preferences. At work, don't hesitate to request tech support or training sessions. The world of work is increasingly digital, and ensuring you have the tools and knowledge to excel is not just beneficial – it's essential for staying relevant and engaged in your role.

As you achieve these milestones, you must recognize and celebrate your accomplishments. Each new skill you acquire, each tech challenge you conquer, deserves acknowledgment. Perhaps you finally set up that smart home device without a hitch or mastered a new software program. Take a moment to pat yourself on the back. Consider sharing your achievements with friends or joining community events celebrating technological success. These gatherings are not only a chance to mingle with like-minded individuals but also an opportunity to inspire others with your journey. Celebrations, whether big or small, fuel your motivation to continue exploring and expanding your tech prowess.

In this digital age, empowerment through technology is not just about keeping up; it's about carving out your niche, finding what excites you, and using technology as a catalyst for personal growth. With the right tools, a dash of determination, and a supportive network, you'll find that the digital landscape isn't a daunting maze but a playground of endless possibilities.

Connecting with Like-Minded Communities

Imagine a place where you can share your passions without leaving the comfort of your armchair. The digital age has made this a delightful reality, offering countless online communities tailored to every interest imaginable. Whether you're a knitting enthusiast, a history buff, or someone who loves discussing travel tales, a forum or social media group awaits you. Finding these like-minded circles begins with a simple search. Platforms like Facebook host myriad groups catering to specific hobbies. For more focused discussions, interest-based forums such as **Reddit** or specialized websites like **Stitch** (source 3) offer spaces designed for individuals over 50, fostering companionship and shared activities. These digital spaces become extensions of our social circles, connecting us with folks who share our enthusiasm and curiosity.

Engaging in these communities can be incredibly rewarding, but it requires a touch of finesse. Imagine stepping into a lively dinner party where everyone is eager to chat. Effective online communication begins with introducing yourself and sharing your interests. Ask open-ended questions to spark discussions, like when talking with a neighbor over the fence. Listen actively and respond thoughtfully; soon, you'll be deeply immersed in meaningful conversations. Community engagement techniques, such as participating in group challenges or contributing to ongoing discussions, help you build connections and establish a presence. These interactions are like planting seeds in a garden; with time and care, they blossom into lasting friendships.

Once you're comfortable, consider sharing your unique knowledge and experiences with your newfound friends. Hosting virtual meetups allows you to bring people together, share stories, or even teach a skill you excel at. It's like organizing a potluck, where everyone brings something to the table. Perhaps you have travel tips to share or a knack for storytelling that can enliven a gathering. Sharing resources and insights enriches the community and enhances your reputation as a valuable member. These activities foster a sense of belonging as you contribute to something larger than yourself.

There's profound satisfaction in being part of a community. It opens doors to supportive feedback networks where ideas are exchanged, and learning is a constant. Imagine having a group of peers ready to offer constructive advice or celebrate your successes. These networks reassure you that you're not alone in your pursuits, offering encouragement when challenges arise. Moreover, community involvement presents numerous collaboration opportunities. Whether co-authoring an article, organizing an event, or simply brainstorming together, these collaborations lead to new experiences and personal growth. The sense of achievement from successfully working with others is fulfilling and inspiring.

Consider creating a resource list of your favorite online communities and groups. Include a brief description of each and why you enjoy them. This can be a handy reference when you're looking to engage or invite others into your circles.

The beauty of connecting with like-minded communities lies in the shared experiences and mutual support they offer. It's about building relationships that enrich our lives and add depth to our everyday activities. In these spaces, you find companionship, laughter, and the joy of exploring interests with others who truly understand. Whether exchanging recipes, discussing the latest book you've read, a great knitting pattern, or planning a virtual trip together, these connections remind us of the simple pleasures and the warmth of shared company.

Sharing Your Knowledge: Teaching Others

Imagine sitting around the dining table with family, the freshly brewed tea filling the air, and the excitement of a new challenge – teaching others about ChatGPT. This isn't just about sharing knowledge; it's an opportunity to illuminate the digital path for those around you. Community workshops are a fantastic avenue for this. Picture a cozy library room filled with eager faces, each person keen to learn how ChatGPT can enhance their daily lives. As you guide them, your confidence grows, and you become the beacon of tech wisdom, gently guiding them into the digital age. Hosting family tech nights can be just as rewarding. Gather the family, perhaps over a potluck dinner, and introduce them to the wonders of AI. Children, parents, and grandparents can all gather around, learning and laughing together. It's a chance to bond, share stories, and explore technology in a relaxed, informal setting.

Teaching is an art, and like any artist, refining your craft is key. Start by considering the diverse learning styles of your audience. Some might be visual learners, and others may be more hands-on. Adapting your teaching methods ensures everyone can follow along. Use engaging lesson plans that include visual aids like diagrams or short videos. Encourage questions and foster an environment where curiosity is welcomed. Remember, teaching isn't about delivering a monologue but sparking a dialogue. Ask open-ended questions and invite participants to share their experiences. This turns a simple lesson into a collaborative exploration, where everyone contributes to the collective understanding. The goal is to create an educational experience as enjoyable as informative.

In this digital age, ChatGPT can be a marvelous teaching aid. It's like having a personal assistant dedicated to your success. Use it to generate content outlines for your sessions, ensuring you cover all the essential topics without missing a beat. Crafting educational quizzes becomes a breeze with ChatGPT's help, allowing you to assess understanding in a fun and engaging way. Imagine the satisfaction of watching participants light up as they realize they've grasped a concept, all thanks to a well-timed quiz question. ChatGPT can also help you prepare for unexpected questions, giving you the confidence to handle any curveballs.

Teaching others is not just about imparting knowledge; it's a powerful way to reinforce your understanding. As you explain concepts to others, you clarify them for yourself, deepening your expertise. Teaching builds confidence in your technological prowess, transforming you from a hesitant user to a seasoned pro. Your understanding broadens, and soon you find yourself not just using ChatGPT but genuinely mastering it. The benefits ripple outwards, too. Those you teach gain confidence and knowledge, sparking their journeys into the digital world. It's a cycle of learning and growth fueled by curiosity and the joy of discovery.

Embrace the opportunity to share your knowledge. Whether in a community center, around the kitchen table, or through online platforms, teaching is a gift you give yourself as much as to others. It's a way to connect, inspire, and create a community of learners, each eager to explore the digital landscape. So, gather your notes, warm up that kettle, and prepare to light the way for others, one lesson at a time.

Personal Growth: Leveraging ChatGPT for Self-Improvement

In the heart of any personal growth endeavor lies a well-crafted plan, like a map guiding you through uncharted territories. With ChatGPT, setting individual development goals becomes an engaging process. Begin by contemplating what areas of your life you'd like to nurture. Whether learning to play the guitar, honing your culinary skills, or diving into digital photography, ChatGPT helps create a structured framework for these aspirations. Use it to break down your goals into manageable steps, ensuring each milestone is achievable and rewarding. Picture this: a digital companion that tracks your progress and celebrates your victories, however small they may be. Progress tracking tools are like modern-day journals, capturing your journey and reminding you how far you've come. Each checkmark is a testament to your dedication, a digital pat on the back that says, "Well done, you're moving forward!"

Self-reflection is another powerful tool in the personal growth toolkit. ChatGPT is the perfect partner for this introspective exercise. Imagine starting each day with quiet contemplation, guided by reflection prompts encouraging you to ponder your thoughts and experiences. These prompts can be as simple as, "What am I grateful for today?" or as deep as, "What lesson did I learn from yesterday's challenges?" Self-awareness exercises help you tune into your inner dialogue, fostering a better understanding of your motivations and desires. By engaging in regular journaling sessions with ChatGPT, you create a safe space for exploring your emotions and thoughts, like a cozy corner where you can unwind and be yourself. This practice clarifies your goals and nurtures a sense of peace and direction in your daily life.

Exploring new areas of interest and acquiring fresh skills is exciting and enriching. ChatGPT is a gateway to boundless possibilities, offering suggestions for hobbies you might never have considered. Always wanted to learn French cooking? ChatGPT can guide you to resources and recipes that transport your taste buds straight to Provence. Interested in exploring career development paths? ChatGPT helps you identify courses and certifications that align with your ambitions. It's like having a personal mentor always ready to offer advice, encouraging you to expand your horizons and step out of your comfort zone. With each new skill you acquire, you add another string to your bow, enhancing your life with layers of knowledge and experience that make every day a little richer.

Recognizing and celebrating personal achievements is vital in maintaining motivation and fostering a sense of accomplishment. Think of personal achievement logs as your hall of fame, where each entry reminds you of your growth and perseverance. Whether mastering a new software program or completing your first 5K run, documenting these successes gives them the recognition they deserve. Reflective celebrations fuel your continued journey, whether shared with family or enjoyed privately. Imagine gathering loved ones for a small celebration, where you share your achievements and the steps you took to reach them. These moments of reflection and acknowledgment are like a warm embrace, reinforcing your belief in your abilities and inspiring you to pursue your next goal with renewed vigor.

The Future of AI: Staying Ahead with ChatGPT

Imagine standing at the brink of a technological dawn where AI is not just a tool but a partner in everyday life. From virtual assistants anticipating your needs to smart appliances adapting to your preferences, AI trends are reshaping how we interact with the world. Emerging technologies like machine learning and neural networks are advancing rapidly, enabling AI to learn and grow intuitively with each interaction. ChatGPT is evolving, too. It's becoming more adept at understanding context and delivering tailored responses, making it a more effective companion in personal and professional settings. Consider ChatGPT's latest updates, including enhanced personalization features and the ability to integrate seamlessly across various platforms. These advancements are paving the way for a future where AI plays a pivotal role in every facet of our lives, from simplifying daily tasks to enriching our social interactions.

Staying informed about these advancements is crucial. Just as you'd keep an ear to the ground for local news, subscribing to AI updates ensures you're always in the loop about new developments. Many resources, from tech blogs to AI newsletters, provide bite-sized insights into the latest trends. Continuous learning is key to remaining relevant in this ever-changing landscape. Online courses can offer structured learning paths, making it easier to grasp complex concepts and apply them in practical scenarios. Embracing lifelong learning in technology keeps your skills sharp. It empowers you to make informed decisions about integrating AI into your life.

With great power comes great responsibility, and that's especially true for AI. As these technologies become more embedded in our daily routines, it's essential to consider the ethical implications. AI systems are only as unbiased as the data they're fed, and understanding these biases is crucial to using AI responsibly. Transparency in AI operations is essential to ensure users know how their data is used and for what purpose. Adhering to responsible usage guidelines ensures that AI is an ally rather than a liability. This includes being mindful of privacy settings and regularly reviewing how your data is collected and stored. As users, advocating for transparency and accountability in AI systems will lead to more ethical practices and trustworthy tools.

The future of AI is bright and full of potential, but it requires curiosity and an open mind. Imagine a world where AI not only assists but inspires new ways of thinking and living. The possibilities are endless, from healthcare innovations that personalize treatment plans to educational tools that adapt to individual learning styles. AI's role in daily life will continue to expand, offering opportunities to enhance creativity, productivity, and connection. By staying curious and exploring these possibilities, you can prepare for a future where AI is integral to your everyday experience.

As we look towards the horizon, consider how these advancements might transform your interactions and enrich the fabric of your life. Embrace this era of innovation with enthusiasm, knowing that you are part of shaping the future landscape with every click and query. Whether through casual conversations with ChatGPT or exploring new AI tools, the discovery journey is exciting and rewarding. This chapter is not just about keeping up with technology; it's about actively participating in the evolution of a world where human ingenuity and artificial intelligence work hand in hand to create something truly remarkable.

Conclusion

Well, my dear reader, we've reached the end of our ChatGPT adventure, and what a journey it's been! From the first tentative steps into the world of AI to the confident strides of a tech-savvy explorer, you've embraced the challenge with the same gusto as learning to ride a bicycle. Like me, you might have started with a few wobbles and a touch of apprehension, but look at you now - navigating the digital landscape like a pro!

Throughout this book, we've uncovered how ChatGPT can enhance our lives. From crafting engaging conversations with grandchildren to planning the perfect road trip, this AI companion has proven to be as versatile as a Swiss Army knife. We've learned to use ChatGPT to bridge generational gaps, fostering connections and shared experiences that transcend age. And let's not forget the joy of discovering new hobbies and interests with ChatGPT as our trusty guide.

But this book is more than just a collection of tips and tricks. It's a testament to the incredible potential of seniors in the digital age. We've shattered the stereotype of the tech-averse elder, proving that curiosity and a willingness to learn know no age limit. By embracing tools like ChatGPT, we've shown that we're not just keeping up with the times – we're shaping them.

As you close this book, I hope you feel empowered to continue your technological journey. The insights and strategies you've gained are just the beginning. Keep exploring, experimenting, and pushing the boundaries of what you thought was possible. Whether you're using ChatGPT to plan a family reunion or to dive into a new creative pursuit, approach each endeavor with the same spirit of adventure that brought you here.

But don't just take my word for it. The real magic happens when you put these lessons into practice. Start small, perhaps by setting up ChatGPT and using it to draft a message to a loved one. As you grow more comfortable, let your imagination run wild. Use ChatGPT to plan a virtual world tour, write a short story, or create a family trivia game. Each small victory will build your confidence and open new doors.

Remember, you're not alone in this journey. As you explore, don't hesitate to reach out and share your experiences. Join online communities, attend workshops, and connect with others who share your passion for learning. The wisdom and support of a shared community can turn any challenge into an opportunity for growth.

As we look to the future, I can't help but feel a sense of excitement. AI is evolving at a breakneck pace, and tools like ChatGPT are just the tip of the iceberg. By embracing these technologies with a curious mind and an open heart, we're not just adapting to change – we're driving it. We're proving that innovation isn't just the domain of the young but the playground of the young at heart.

So, my dear reader, as you embark on your next adventure, know that I'm cheering you on every step of the way.

Your journey is a testament to our generation's incredible resilience, creativity, and wit. Keep learning, laughing, and showing the world what we're made of.

And remember, if a tech-challenged grandmother of four like me can become a ChatGPT aficionado, there's no limit to what you can achieve. The future is bright, and with ChatGPT by your side, you're ready to make it yours.

Happy exploring!

Margaret

References

- Elite Care Health Centers. (n.d.). ChatGPT for seniors: How AI can transform seniors' lives. Elite Care. https://www.elitecarehc.com/blog/chatgpt-for-seniors-how-ai-can-transform-seniors-lives/
- Microsoft Data Science. (2023, April 19). How large language models work: From zero to ChatGPT. Medium. https://medium.com/data-science-at-microsoft/how-large-language-models-work-91c362f5b78f
- Tettra. (n.d.). How to sign up for ChatGPT (step-by-step guide). Tettra. https://tettra.com/article/how-to-sign-up-for-chatgpt/
- Algolia. (2023, February 14). Debunking the most common AI myths. Algolia Blog. https://www.algolia.com/blog/ai/debunking-the-most-common-ai-myths
- Cubed. (2023, May 24). ChatGPT's role in scheduling, reminders, and to-do lists. Cubed Blog. https://cubed.run/blog/organizing-made-easy-chatg

pts-role-in-scheduling-reminders-and-to-do-lists

- Gartenberg, C. (2023, May 5). I handed over meal planning to ChatGPT. It paid off big time. CNET. https://www.cnet.com/home/kitchen-and-household/i-handed-over-meal-planning-to-chatgpt-it-paid-off-big-time/

- Coveo. (2023, March 28). From aisles to algorithms: The impact of AI on grocery shopping. Coveo Blog. https://www.coveo.com/blog/impact-of-ai-on-grocery-shopping/

- Taylor, E. (2023, June 7). Automating household chores with ChatGPT: A comprehensive guide. Medium. https://emiliotaylor.medium.com/automating-household-chores-with-chatgpt-a-comprehensive-guide-8137a5b10b79

- AARP. (2023, May 12). How to talk to your kids and grandkids about AI. AARP. https://www.aarp.org/home-family/personal-technology/info-2023/ai-kids-grandkids.html

- Schuitema, W. (2023, July 11). Top 10 AI apps for family activity management. Warren Schuitema. https://warrenschuitema.com/post/top-10-ai-apps-for-family-activity-management

- AI Genealogy Insights. (2023, March 17). Using ChatGPT to write stories from family trees, create trees from stories. AI Genealogy Insights. https://aigenealogyinsights.com/2023/03/17/artificial-intelligence-and-genealogy-using-chatgpt-to-write-stories-from-family-trees-create-trees-from-stories/

- Quora. (n.d.). How does ChatGPT handle user input

that contains slang or colloquialisms? Quora. https://www.quora.com/How-does-ChatGPT-handle-user-input-that-contains-slang-or-colloquialisms

- Goodwings. (2023, June 2). How to use ChatGPT to build a travel itinerary. Goodwings Blog. https://blog.goodwings.com/how-to-use-chatgpt-to-build-a-travel-itinerary

- Microsoft. (2023, August 8). How to use AI to help you pack for vacation. Microsoft 365 Life Hacks. https://www.microsoft.com/en-us/microsoft-365-life-hacks/organization/how-to-use-ai-to-help-you-pack-for-vacation

- Google. (n.d.). Google Translate. Google Play. https://play.google.com/store/apps/details?id=com.google.android.apps.translate26hl=en_US

- Travelpayouts. (2023, May 18). Unlocking the power of AI in content creation for travel bloggers. Travelpayouts Blog. https://www.travelpayouts.com/blog/unlocking-the-power-of-ai-in-content-creation-for-travel-bloggers/

- The Digital Speaker. (2023, March 3). Privacy in the age of AI: Risks, challenges and solutions. The Digital Speaker. https://www.thedigitalspeaker.com/privacy-age-ai-risks-challenges-solutions/

- PasswordManager.com. (2025, January 15). The best password managers for seniors of 2025. PasswordManager.com. https://www.passwordmanager.com/best-password-managers-for-seniors/

- Timus Networks. (2023, April 12). What is two-factor

authentication (2FA)? How it works. Timus Networks. https://www.timusnetworks.com/understanding-two-factor-authentication-2fa-and-its-importance-for-enhancing-security/

- Guildhawk. (2023, February 22). ChatGPT security best practices: A comprehensive guide. Guildhawk Blog. https://www.guildhawk.com/blog/ensuring-the-security-of-chatgpt-a-comprehensive-guide
- Autumn View Gardens Ellisville. (2023, June 9). 28 writing and journaling prompts for older adults. Autumn View Gardens Blog. https://www.autumnviewgardensellisville.com/blog/28-writing-and-journaling-prompts-for-older-adults
- SeniorLiving.org. (2023, April 19). 9 brain games to stay sharp and improve memory. SeniorLiving.org. https://www.seniorliving.org/life/brain-games/
- 55places. (2023, January 20). The ultimate hobby guide: 50 hobbies for seniors. 55places Blog. https://www.55places.com/blog/the-ultimate-hobby-guide-50-hobbies-for-seniors
- The Bristal Assisted Living. (2023, July 7). The best apps and tools for seniors to learn a new language. The Bristal Blog. https://blog.thebristal.com/the-best-apps-and-tools-for-seniors-to-learn-a-new-language
- Senior Planet. (n.d.). Online classes for seniors. AARP Senior Planet. https://seniorplanet.org/classes/
- University of Massachusetts Amherst. (n.d.). Creating effective online quizzes and exams. UMass Amherst IDEAS.

https://www.umass.edu/ideas/creating-effective-online-quizzes-and-exams

- Marr, B. (2023, May 30). 10 amazing real-world examples of how companies are using ChatGPT in 2023. Forbes. https://www.forbes.com/sites/bernardmarr/2023/05/30/10-amazing-real-world-examples-of-how-companies-are-using-chatgpt-in-2023/
- Instructional Design Australia. (2023, June 15). 10 engaging learning activities to enhance retention in adult education. Instructional Design Australia. https://instructionaldesign.com.au/10-engaging-learning-activities-to-enhance-retention-in-adult-education/
- Skills You Need. (n.d.). Overcoming technology anxiety: A guide for seniors. SkillsYouNeed. https://www.skillsyouneed.com/rhubarb/overcoming-technology-anxiety.html
- Design Bootcamp. (2023, January 25). When grandma met AI: A case study on ChatGPT. Medium. https://medium.com/design-bootcamp/when-grandma-met-ai-48907392e796
- Stitch. (n.d.). Stitch: The social community for anyone over 50. Stitch. https://www.stitch.net/
- OpenAI. (n.d.). ChatGPT release notes. OpenAI Help Center. https://help.openai.com/en/articles/6825453-chatgpt-release-notes

ChatGPT Café Glossary of Terms

Your Friendly Tech Dictionary

AI (Artificial Intelligence)
A computer's ability to do things that normally require human intelligence - like learning, problem-solving, or chatting with you over coffee!

Algorithm
A fancy word for a set of instructions a computer follows to solve a problem or perform a task - like a recipe, but for machines.

ChatGPT
Your helpful virtual assistant, trained by OpenAI, designed to respond to questions, generate text, and help with just about anything you can imagine. Think of it as your digital barista - ready to serve ideas on demand.

Prompt
The question or instruction you type in to get ChatGPT

hatGPT started. The better your prompt, the better the response - like giving your barista just the right coffee order.

Token
A piece of text that ChatGPT uses to understand your request. A word might be one token or split into several, depending on length. (You don't have to count them - just know there's a limit per conversation.)

Training Data
The collection of text from books, websites, and more that ChatGPT learned from. It doesn't "know" the world like a person, but it's great at patterns and conversation.

Model
The version of ChatGPT you're using. Newer models (like GPT-4) are more advanced and better at understanding context than earlier ones.

OpenAI
The organization behind ChatGPT, focused on creating safe and useful AI tools for everyone.

Interface
The screen or program where you type and see ChatGPT's responses. Kind of like your favorite café window - the place where the magic gets served up.

Context
What ChatGPT remembers from earlier in the conversation. It helps keep the chat smooth, like a good server remembering your usual order.

Natural Language Processing (NLP)
The techy term for how computers understand and generate human language. It's what makes talking to ChatGPT feel... well, natural!

Chat History
A log of your previous conversations with ChatGPT - handy if you want to review past chats or continue where you left off.

Creative Mode vs. Precise Mode
Some versions of ChatGPT let you choose between more imaginative or more factual responses. Choose based on your mood - espresso or chamomile?

Knowledge Cutoff
The date when ChatGPT stopped learning new info. For example, if the cutoff is June 2024, it won't know what happened after that.

Multimodal
A version of ChatGPT that can understand both text and images (like showing it a photo of your handwritten note and asking for help with it).

User Interface (UI)
The buttons, boxes, and menus you interact with. A good UI makes tech feel easy - like a well-designed café menu.

BONUS Chapter

ChatGPT Café Cat

A Little Extra For You

You've made it this far – brewing ideas, exploring prompts, and finding new ways to spark creativity. Consider this next section your bonus refill: a gift of extra prompts and inspiration, waiting to be unlocked with just a quick scan or click.

Think of it as your "secret menu" at the ChatGPT Café – something a little special for readers like you who are curious enough to peek behind the counter. Whether you're sipping slowly through one prompt at a time or diving in for a full creative feast, this bonus chapter is here to keep the conversation flowing.

Go ahead – follow the link (or scan the code) and discover what's waiting for you. Your next adventure in the Café begins here.

https://tinyurl.com/ChatGPTCafeBonus

Done is better
than perfect.
Especially when
there's coffee
involved.

Breadcrumbs

*****REVIEW

YES – You REALLY Did It!
You've officially stepped into the fascinating world of ChatGPT – curiosity, courage, and all! Whether you're impressing the grandkids with a clever AI trick, finally feeling at home in a digital world that once felt like Mars, or just having fun exploring new prompts, you're rocking it.

But here's the best part: you're not done yet (don't worry, no homework involved!).

You can help others take that same exciting first step by sharing your thoughts about this book. Your review might be the exact nudge someone else over fifty needs to say, "If they can do it, maybe I can too!"

Think of it as leaving a trail of coffee beans – or maybe a plate of chocolate chip cookies – so fellow beginners feel welcome to join the ChatGPT Café.

By leaving a quick review, you're helping to:

Spark curiosity and confidence in other over-fifty beginners

Keep the AI magic going strong

Build a warm, supportive community of learners

Thank you for being part of the journey. The real magic of AI isn't just in what ChatGPT can do – it's in how we share what we've learned, passing it along like stories over a cozy cup of coffee.

Please leave your honest review on the platform where you found this book.

With gratitude (and a celebratory chair dance),
Margaret Fields

Made in United States
Orlando, FL
10 September 2026

87554636R00087